User-generated Content and Its Impact on Web-based Library Services

Chandos
Information Professional Series

Series Editor: Ruth Rikowski
(e-mail: Rikowskigr@aol.com)

Chandos' new series of books are aimed at the busy information professional. They have been specially commissioned to provide the reader with an authoritative view of current thinking. They are designed to provide easy-to-read and (most importantly) practical coverage of topics that are of interest to librarians and other information professionals. If you would like a full listing of current and forthcoming titles, please visit our website www.chandospublishing.com or e-mail info@chandospublishing.com or telephone +44 (0) 1223 891358.

New authors: we are always pleased to receive ideas for new titles; if you would like to write a book for Chandos, please contact Dr Glyn Jones on e-mail gjones@chandospublishing.com or telephone number +44 (0) 1993 848726.

Bulk orders: some organisations buy a number of copies of our books. If you are interested in doing this, we would be pleased to discuss a discount. Please e-mail info@chandospublishing.com or telephone +44 (0) 1223 891358.

User-generated Content and Its Impact on Web-based Library Services

Kay Cahill

Chandos Publishing
Oxford · Cambridge · New Delhi

Chandos Publishing
TBAC Business Centre
Avenue 4
Station Lane
Witney
Oxford OX28 4BN
UK
Tel: +44 (0) 1993 848726
E-mail: info@chandospublishing.com
www.chandospublishing.com

Chandos Publishing is an imprint of Woodhead Publishing Limited

Woodhead Publishing Limited
Abington Hall
Granta Park
Great Abington
Cambridge CB21 6AH
UK
www.woodheadpublishing.com

First published in 2009

ISBN:
978 1 84334 534 3

British Library Cataloguing-in-Publication Data.
A catalogue record for this book is available from the British Library.

Typeset in the UK by Concerto.
Printed in the UK and USA.

Contents

List of figures

About the author

Kay Cahill is the senior librarian for website and community development at Vancouver Public Library, Canada. Kay graduated from the Information Studies program at the University of Wales, Aberystwyth, before moving to Canada in 2004. She joined Vancouver Public Library in 2005 and has been responsible for a variety of portfolios, including staff and public IT training and the library's virtual reference service. Most recently she was part of the project management team for the 2008 redesign and relaunch of www.vpl.ca.

Kay has been published in a number of professional journals on topics including assistive technology in libraries, the impact of Google and Web 2.0 on library services and the changing nature of the information profession. She is a regular speaker at Canadian library conferences, such as the British Columbia Library Association Conference and the Netspeed Technology Conference.

With 15 years' experience in the library and information profession in the UK and Canada, Kay is a leading advocate for the strategic implementation of new web technologies to enhance library services and the development and delivery of library services in the online space.

In her spare time Kay is a keen skier, swimmer, hiker and cyclist, and enjoys exploring remote areas of BC. She is very happily married and loves living on the West Coast.

List of acronyms

API	application programming interface
BBS	bulletin board system
BC	British Columbia
CCG	Chinese Canadian Genealogy
CMS	content management system
CPL	Cheshire Public Library
CSS	cascading style sheets
DPL	Denver Public Library
EE	Expression Engine
ESL	English as a second language
FAQ	frequently asked question
GPS	global positioning system
HCL	Hennepin County Library
ILS	integrated library system
ISBN	International Standard Book Number
KPI	key performance indicator
LoC	Library of Congress
MT	Moveable Type
OPL	Oakville Public Library

RSA	Royal Society of Arts, Manufactures and Commerce
RSS	really simple syndication
TPL	Toronto Public Library
VPL	Vancouver Public Library

1

The information environment

Web 2.0

It was 2004 when the buzz around Web 2.0 really started to build: the time when the internet effectively came of age, moving from a loose collection of websites to a genuine computing platform supporting the principles of collaboration, creativity, socializing and sharing. Web 2.0, in other words, was about the user-generated web: a brave new world where becoming an author was as easy as coming up with a username and password for LiveJournal, Blogger or Vox, and the purpose of publishing was not just to reach an audience but to encourage that audience to talk back, to debate and challenge the content in front of them.

The phrase Web 2.0 has been bandied around so much since then that it's become a cliché, or worse, meaningless. Google 'define: Web 2.0' and you'll come up with several screens of definitions, most of which include words like 'proposed', 'perceived' and 'supposed' and talk about an ongoing transition of the web as we know it. Web 2.0, it seems, is as much about characteristics and trends as it is about specific tools and software. O'Reilly Media, which coined the term Web 2.0 at a 2004 technology conference, summarizes it effectively:

> Web 2.0 refers to a perceived second-generation of Web-based services – such as social networking sites,

> wikis, communication tools, and folksonomies – that emphasize online collaboration and sharing among users. It is a model that is genuinely interactive, where end users upload as well as download.[1]

Web 2.0 is about flexibility, portability and collaboration. It's about creating tools and services that enable us to move data easily around the web, repurposing and aggregating them as needed. And more than anything else, it's about platforms that allow us to collaborate: wikis, blogs, media-sharing sites and social networking communities. It's about turning the information that's presented on the web into a dialogue rather than a lecture.

Understandably, this concept is resulting in some quite radical changes in the ways that public libraries – the gatekeepers of information in its more traditional formats – develop and promote their services. In the early days of the web, the challenge was in building a web presence in the first place. Now, things have changed. Our core users have evolved: they are no longer new to the internet, navigating with uncertainty and hesitation. They are – for the most part – tech savvy and IT literate, and they expect nothing less than the highest standards from the library's website. Our services have evolved: increasingly, public libraries are managing large and complex collections of electronic resources, and bringing traditional core services online using tools such as live chat reference. Information management has evolved: content management systems and database-driven websites offer more flexible and efficient ways to control content production and appearance. And most importantly, the internet has evolved. Web 2.0 offers libraries the opportunity to engage users in new ways, bringing the expertise that exists in the community into the library and enabling user opinion and feedback to drive not just our content, but our direction.

This, of course, is a sea change for a profession that has relied on a foundation of tried-and-tested control systems, classification schemata and clearly defined definitions of authority. The information environment has evolved almost beyond recognition in the past 15 years, and the lines that we were taught to trust in library school are shifting and blurring beneath our feet. The pace of change in libraries and librarianship has traditionally been slow, and now we're having to balance the need to respond and react quickly enough to remain relevant in this rapidly changing environment with the equally important need for thoughtful evaluation of new technologies and information delivery mechanisms to ensure we're really enhancing our services rather than simply jumping on the latest bandwagon. It's certainly an interesting time to be a librarian.

To set the scene for the impact that Web 2.0 is having on libraries and library websites, we'll take a brief tour of some of the tools, technologies and trends that have been instrumental in the coming of age of this new generation of web services and the evolution of the current information environment.

Brief history of blogging

Blogging was the first Web 2.0 tool really to hit the mainstream. The term 'blog' comes from the original descriptor 'weblog', used to describe online journals in the very early days of such tools. An early blogger then broke the term into 'we blog', with blog becoming both a verb describing the process of writing and a noun describing the journal itself.

The early impact of blogging was much like the inception of war reporting in the Crimea, or the poems that found their way back from the trenches during the First World War. Blogging was – and is – a direct report from the front lines, an often deeply personal interpretation of events with a significant historic or political impact. Long before emo kids had discovered the joys of sharing their teen angst via the net, political blogs and war blogs had begun to make a mark on the public consciousness. Blogs provide an instant dissemination of personal observations and experiences, coloured by individual experience and perception rather than the typical spin that characterizes media reports. For a populace sick to death of newspaper conglomerates and media hype, blogs were a refreshing change.

The other unique aspect of blogs was that they enabled more or less instant feedback (in some cases barring a brief delay for approval by the blog owners) on the part of the reader. If part of a story didn't ring true, the reader could challenge the author directly. If readers had their own observations on the event, they could build on the original post and share their experiences. The blog became a dialogue, a conversation between author and audience, a forum for discussion and opinion sharing among people who need not share the same social circle or even live on the same side of the globe.

The earliest blogs were simply chronological posts on individual websites. The first blog-specific software was OpenDiary (www.opendiary.com), which launched in 1998. It was OpenDiary that introduced the dialogue component to blogs by enabling the posting of comments, and comment responses, for the first time. It was followed in short order by LiveJournal (www.livejournal.com), which originated via a university student's efforts to stay in touch with his friends, and Blogger (www.blogger.com), another of the current giants of the blogging world. LiveJournal was the first blogging software to incorporate communities, where like-minded users could gather based on interests rather than mutual 'friends'; these communities were a precursor of the social networking phenomenon that was later to sweep the internet.

More recently, publishing software such as WordPress and Typepad has seen the largest boom in popularity. These platforms differ from straightforward blogging software in a number of ways, primarily in that they enable the creation of 'pages' that exist outside of the blog chronology. This allows them to be used as a mini content management system for sites, as the blog can become an embedded feature of a significantly larger website, all controlled and managed through the same software.

Today OpenDiary is still ticking along, with 555,520 online diaries registered; LiveJournal has expanded beyond all recognition, changed hands several times and now boasts 16.2 million registered journals and approximately 160,000 individual blog entries per day (Figure 1.1); and Blogger was

Figure 1.1 LiveJournal, August 2008

Source: www.livejournal.com

purchased by Google in 2003, and by 2007 was ranked number 16 in terms of unique visitors to domains.[2] WordPress.com, the hosted version of WordPress's open source publishing software, has 3.8 million blogs registered and around 150,000 entries posted per day (Figure 1.2).[3]

In addition to hosted blogging solutions like LiveJournal and Blogger, millions of users also build and host their own blogs. There are many other dedicated blogging platforms out there, and most content management systems now include a blogging module as a standard feature. Blogs are also built into many social networking sites like MySpace, enabling even more users to share their thoughts online. There are blogs based around politics, current events, products, trends, hobbies, random obsessions: no matter what the topic, somewhere on the net there's a blog about it.

An interesting recent trend is the microblog, typified by Twitter (www.twitter.com). The idea of a microblog is that posts are limited to a very short length – in Twitter's case, just 140 characters – and are intended to make it easier for people to stay up to date with each other's lives via very brief updates that are quick and easy both to post and to read. Critics argue that microblogging is a further example of how the internet is reducing attention spans and dumbing down content, but the format has clearly struck a chord with users; Twitter has expanded to the point where its frequent outages and other technical difficulties are a source of great frustration to dedicated tweeters, and the 'fail whale' (Figure 1.3) has become a synonym for poor performance both online and offline.

Figure 1.2 WordPress, early August 2008

3,805,814 BLOGS, 145,999 NEW POSTS, 49,313,484 WORDS TODAY.

Source: www.wordpress.com

Figure 1.3 Twitter's fail whale

Technorati's annual 'State of the blogosphere' for 2007 reported that the site was tracking 70 million blogs, with approximately 1.4 new blogs created every second – that's around 120,000 new blogs per day.[4] It should be noted that while this number is startling enough, it is already more than a year old and does not include 'in-house' blogs on websites such as MySpace, which offer an embedded blog as part of each user's personal page, or microblogs like Twitter. The true number of blogs, like the number of pages on the internet, may not be a figure that we're able to pin down, but it's certainly getting exponentially higher and will have increased by a couple of dozen in the time it took you to read this paragraph.

World of wikis

A wiki is a collaborative software tool that allows the creation of webpages which can be edited and modified by multiple users. In addition to allowing input from many users, wikis use a simple protocol to create links between pages, making it quick and easy for users to browse between topics (Figure 1.4).

Most wikis use a combination of simple mark-up language and HTML to allow basic formatting of pages. The nature of wikis means that their content is constantly evolving, but most wiki models maintain a history of pages

Figure 1.4 Too quick and easy? The problem with Wikipedia

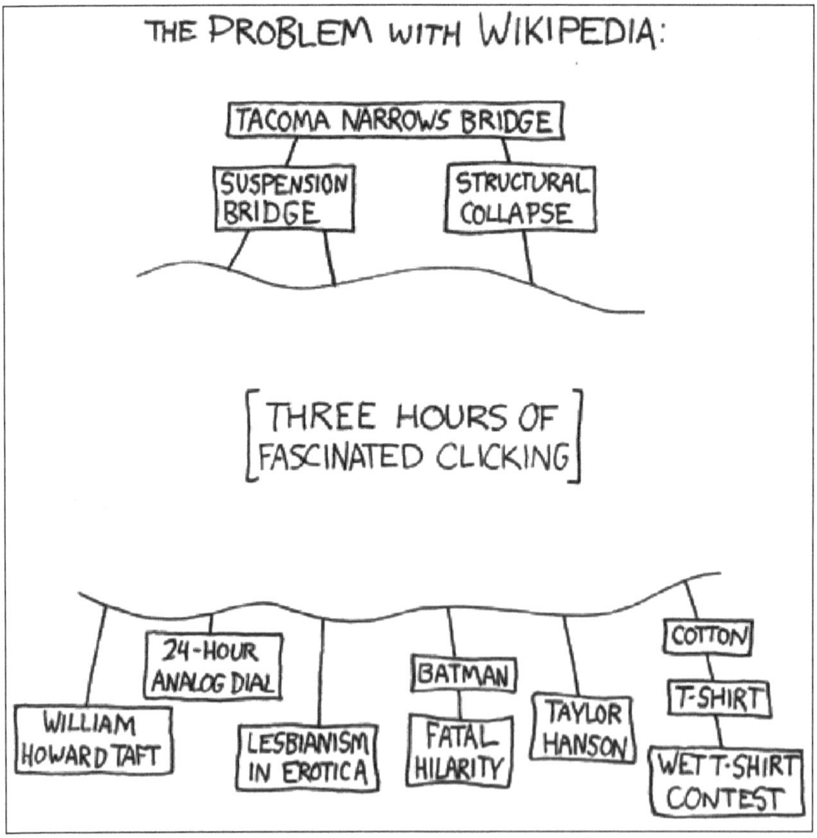

Source: http://xkcd.com/214/, courtesy of Randall Munroe

that allows reversion to a previous iteration if erroneous content (or other issues) is identified with a current version.

Depending on the needs of the owner, some wikis (especially those owned by private businesses) require user authentication to edit pages, but many are open to all. The concept of open, collaborative content creation and editing remains absolutely core to the wiki, and has become such a cultural meme that authors Don Tapscott and Anthony Williams chose the title *Wikinomics* for their fascinating look at how a new, collaborative model is driving innovation and success in the global economy.[5] (In true collaborative style, Tapscott and Williams ran an open discussion to allow the public to choose the title of the book. *Wikinomics* won out over contenders that included *The Power of Us*, *Edit this Book!* and *(Your Input Needed Here)*.)

The first wiki, WikiWikiWeb, was launched in 1995 and the advantages of the format became immediately obvious, with companies seizing on its potential for communication and collaboration in running projects, creating and maintaining documentation, and forming the basis for a new breed of collaborative intranet. Now there are dozens of wiki software packages to choose from, including open source and licensed models. Popular wiki options include MediaWiki, Twiki, DokuWiki and PBWiki.

Wikipedia (www.wikipedia.org), of course, is the wiki that cemented the place of this particular read/write platform on the open web. Founded by Jimmy Wales and Larry Sanger in 2001, Wikipedia was originally launched as a side project to Nupedia, an online encyclopedia that followed the more traditional peer-reviewed model. With little more restriction on contribution than the requirement for a non-biased point of view, the wiki-based Wikipedia expanded to the point where it eventually consumed

Nupedia, with the latter being discontinued and its content added to the ever-growing article base on Wikipedia in 2003. Today, Wikipedia features more than 10 million articles in 253 languages.[6]

Wikipedia is no longer quite as open as it was in its early days. A team of administrators moderate the articles; while they have no ability to interfere in specific disputes, they are able to lock articles to prevent further editing, prevent specific users from editing and delete articles. Detailed policies and guidelines have sprung up to encourage contributors to remain true to the spirit of Wikipedia, perhaps the most informative of which is 'What Wikipedia is not'.[7]

- Wikipedia is not a paper encyclopedia.
- Wikipedia is not a dictionary.
- Wikipedia is not a publisher of original thought.
- Wikipedia is not a soapbox.
- Wikipedia is not a mirror or a repository of links, images or media files.
- Wikipedia is not a blog, webspace provider or social networking or memorial site.
- Wikipedia is not a directory.
- Wikipedia is not a manual, guidebook or textbook.
- Wikipedia is not a crystal ball.
- Wikipedia is not an indiscriminate collection of information.
- Wikipedia is not censored.
- Wikipedia is not a bureaucracy.
- Wikipedia is not governed by statute.
- Wikipedia is not a battleground.

- Wikipedia is not an anarchy.
- Wikipedia is not your web host.

Wikipedia's open editing model has inevitably led to criticism and questions of bias, reliability and authority (Figure 1.5). Some articles have been so repeatedly vandalized (an often-cited example is the biography of George W. Bush) that they remain permanently in a protected state, either blocked from general editing or locked down so that users attempting to register the article have their IP address logged and their changes approved before they are visible on the site. Many schools and universities discourage students from using Wikipedia as a source, and those of us who have spent substantial amounts of time staffing live reference services or children's reference desks have grown used to the K–12 age group reporting 'Not Wikipedia; my teacher says I can't use it.'

Nonetheless, Wikipedia's articles stand up surprisingly well in testing. A 2005 study by *Nature* compared

Figure 1.5 Wikipedian protestor

Source: http://xkcd.com/285/, courtesy of Randall Munroe

Wikipedia directly with the *Encyclopaedia Britannica*, and found that the number of significant inaccuracies was even across the two platforms, with minor inaccuracies only a fraction higher on Wikipedia.[8] Wikipedia has an estimated 75,000 regular editors,[9] many of whom have thousands upon thousands of publications, edits and corrections to their names. Where an inaccuracy exists, a legion of eager contributors are waiting to correct it. When a vandal repeatedly sabotages an article, experienced editors are poised to add that article or that user to their watch lists, and prevent further incidents. Wikipedia has numerous safeguards built in to protect the integrity and accuracy of its articles, and the rigorous checking by surveys such as the one carried out in *Nature* indicates that these do go a long way towards ensuring a high level of accuracy, regardless of concerns over the distributed nature of the contribution model.

Dialogue and discussion: forums and bulletin boards

The early adoption and subsequent endurance of discussion forums are a testimony to people's desire to connect and converse with each other online. Long before commercial internet was available – as far back as the 1970s – users equipped with little more than a baud modem and a phone line were interacting using dial-in bulletin board systems (BBSs). The earliest BBSs were usually run as hobbies by individual users, quite often out of a spare bedroom or even a closet, and offered little in the way of sophistication: messages could be exchanged in plain text, basic software uploaded and downloaded at painfully slow speeds, and users could play simple online games with one another.

Usenet, a network communication system established in 1980, gathered news articles and responses together in a collection of subject-based newsgroups. This allowed users to subscribe to topics of interest and engage in discussion about particular articles by posting responses that would be gathered together in a thread, enabling other users to follow and participate in the ongoing conversation. Usenet has been archived by Google, and searching its early threads is a fascinating study in the evolution of online dialogue.

On the modern internet, the discussion forum has become entirely ubiquitous. Most content management systems now offer a discussion forum module that can be bolted on to virtually any site, or users can set up forums using flexible and portable software like the PHP bulletin boards. 'Discussion' is inherent in a majority of websites of significant size, whether it's help forums for software users or the ability to comment on news stories.

Discussion forums tend not to exist in isolation: they generally build up around a specific topic or set of topics. Discussion boards that are completely general in nature end up being little more than glorified chatrooms; one of the greatest challenges for the owners or moderators of topic-specific discussion forums is ensuring that conversation stays on topic. Most discussion boards require registration and have a general set of rules and expected behaviors, or netiquette, to which users agree to conform when they first sign up. Ensuring that these rules are followed usually requires moderation in some capacity, either by the site owner or by a group of moderators or administrators who have the ability to remove off-topic or abusive posts, issue warnings and in some cases remove or suspend user accounts.

Because of the relatively free-flowing nature of the conversation on discussion forums, they are one of the user-generated content formats that suffer most from abuse, and consequently require the most active moderation. Flamewars are common on larger discussion boards, where a thread descends into a series of insults hurled between any number of users. Discussion boards are also perfect grounds for trolls: users who have no interest in genuine discussion on a topic, but instead post inflammatory, derogatory or abusive comments with the sole intention of stirring up as much trouble on the site as possible. Alias accounts, where a single user sets up multiple accounts with different names, are also common on discussion boards. It can be an enormous challenge for forum owners to find a balance between moderating to a degree where abuse does not spoil the site and overmoderating to a point where the community tire of the restrictions on their dialogue and seek another venue. While these issues are by no means unique to discussion boards, they are certainly exacerbated by the free-flowing nature of the dialogue.

That said, discussion forums remain an enormously flexible, popular tool for engaging in conversation online. They can also be a great tool for tapping into the wisdom of the masses. Open source software communities rely extensively on discussion forums to share information, troubleshoot problems and work on new features and enhancements. It's often quicker and easier (not to mention cheaper!) to get a response on a software forum from someone who has already worked through the same issue than it is to wait, or pay, for formal technical support.

Various sites have experimented with the idea of a discussion board as a human encyclopedia: early efforts such as WHquestion and KnowPost offered access to human subject experts through the medium of a question-and-answer-based discussion format. The popularity of current Q&A giant Yahoo! Answers (http://answers.yahoo.com/), which reports over 60 million users[10] and a 75 per cent market share of online Q&A traffic,[11] indicates that this is still an enormously popular means of seeking answers online – even though a quick trawl through recently posted questions reveals answers that range from the absurd to the ridiculous, and in some cases the blatantly wrong. The most interesting thing about Yahoo! Answers is that it lends a degree of proof to the fact that some people would rather seek information through connections with other people, even when the quality of that information is extremely variable, than from traditional sources.

Facebook, MySpace and the rise of the social network

One thing that the popularity of all the tools listed above – blogs, wikis, bulletin boards, discussion forums and Q&A sites – shows is that, more than anything else, people have a desire to connect and engage with each other. Even though the social networking explosion on the internet is a relatively recent phenomenon, driven by the twin behemoths of MySpace and Facebook, it was an inevitable development that was only ever waiting for the right tools to emerge to power it.

Online social networks use a variety of mechanisms to connect people through both real and virtual contacts. For example, Facebook (www.facebook.com) and MySpace (www.myspace.com) allow you to search your e-mail contacts list to find people who are already registered on the site. LinkedIn (www.linkedin.com), an industry-based social networking site, uses your current and former workplaces to build a network of professional connections. Facebook networks allow you to connect with people in your immediate geographical area, and most social networking sites also suggest people you may know based on, for example, mutual friends, workplaces or other criteria.

The rise of the social network has been incredibly fast. The first foray into modern social networking was Friendster (www.friendster.com), which launched in 2002, but the Friendster model failed to anticipate the phenomenal growth of the site and technical difficulties, predominantly very slow page load times, cost it much of its momentum. (Friendster is still around and still has quite a respectable user base, but primarily draws this from the Philippines; it has lost its global reach.) Into this gap stepped MySpace, which launched in 2003 and was the site that propelled social networking into the mainstream. MySpace was founded by a group of employees at eUniverse, including MySpace CEO Chris de Wolfe and president Tom Anderson (the ubiquitous Tom who appears on every single MySpace user's friends list when they first join), and was designed to fill the same social networking niche as Friendster.

MySpace users can create fully customizable profiles from which they can build networks of friends, post photos, videos and blog updates and share personal information. Within three years MySpace was boasting more than 100 million users, and it is still growing at a rate of almost quarter of a million new users per day.[12] It has not been without its critics (in fact, it was named the worst website on the internet by *PC World* magazine in 2006 for a combination of its security flaws and horrendous accessibility problems[13]), but there is no doubt that the simplicity of its interface and the range of features it offers struck an immediate chord with internet users, especially those of school age. The ease of setting up pages and uploading music and video has also made it a popular option with both signed and unsigned bands looking to promote their music. MySpace was purchased by Rupert Murdoch's media network News Corporation for US$580 million in mid-2005.

The rival to the social networking throne is Facebook, founded by Harvard University student Mark Zuckerburg. Facebook launched a year later than MySpace, in 2004, and has now edged ahead of its predecessor in terms of unique traffic.[14] Initially Facebook was only open to college students, which restricted its potential user base significantly, but since opening its doors to anyone with a valid e-mail address in September 2006 it has launched a significant challenge to MySpace's previously effortless dominance of the social networking space. Facebook offers many of the same features – unique profile pages, embedded video, photo hosting – but in a much cleaner, more utilitarian layout with far fewer customization options. After opening its API to developers in 2007 a rash of third-party applications started to take the site in a more cluttered, MySpacey direction, but Facebook reconfirmed its commitment to a clean and streamlined look and feel with a 2008 redesign that relegated the applications to a tab on the navigation bar.

Like MySpace, Facebook also has its issues. Privacy is a significant concern, and the site was forced to withdraw its planned Beacon advertising service in late 2007 following a huge user protest. Beacon's purpose was to take data relating to a Facebook user's activity from third-party websites – for example, the purchase of items on eBay – and then share them on their Facebook Wall. The argument was that this would allow targeted third-party advertising and increased sharing of user activity, with the twist that it was an opt-out rather than opt-in system – users who took no action would automatically have their data shared whether they wanted it to happen or not. Facebook users universally recoiled in horror at what they saw as a massive invasion of their personal privacy, and the company subsequently made the product opt in rather than opt out and issued a formal apology. The growing intrusion of advertising on Facebook remains an issue, as does the increasing presence of third-party applications. While some of these offer excellent functional enhancements to the user experience, others are little more than garish decoration and high-school-style popularity contests, which users grumble would be better suited to the more teen-oriented MySpace.

Regardless of these issues, Facebook's user base has expanded enormously since the site opened its doors to the general populace in 2006. It now has more than 100 million active users[15] and is growing by more than 200,000 users per day.[16]

Interestingly, one of the key areas in which Facebook appears to be well ahead in its battle for social networking dominance is the ease with which it allows people to establish connections with real, as well as virtual, friends. MySpace has never entirely recovered from its early treatment as a teenage popularity contest, when the goal was simply to build as large a friends list as possible regardless of whether or not the individual user had any real connection with those people. Facebook is built around offline networks – schools, colleges, workplaces, e-mail contact lists – and designed to enable quick and easy connections with people in those networks. It also allows people to set up groups to which they can invite their friends, and create events pages and mail invitations. MySpace is about the quick-and-dirty virtual connection; Facebook is about building virtual relationships with real-life connections. MySpace, with its overcrowded profiles, inconsistent look and feel and armies of loosely connected friends, very much reflects its initial uptake among teenage users; Facebook occupies a different niche, and currently looks to have successfully positioned itself as 'MySpace for grown-ups'.

There are, of course, hundreds of other social networking sites (Figure 1.6) competing for a share of the space that is currently dominated by MySpace and Facebook, and it will be interesting to see if any of these can mount a serious challenge. Google's social networking service, Orkut (www.orkut.com), is gaining in popularity and will definitely be one to watch over the next year or so.

Figure 1.6 xkcd's map of online communities (created prior to Facebook's explosion in popularity)

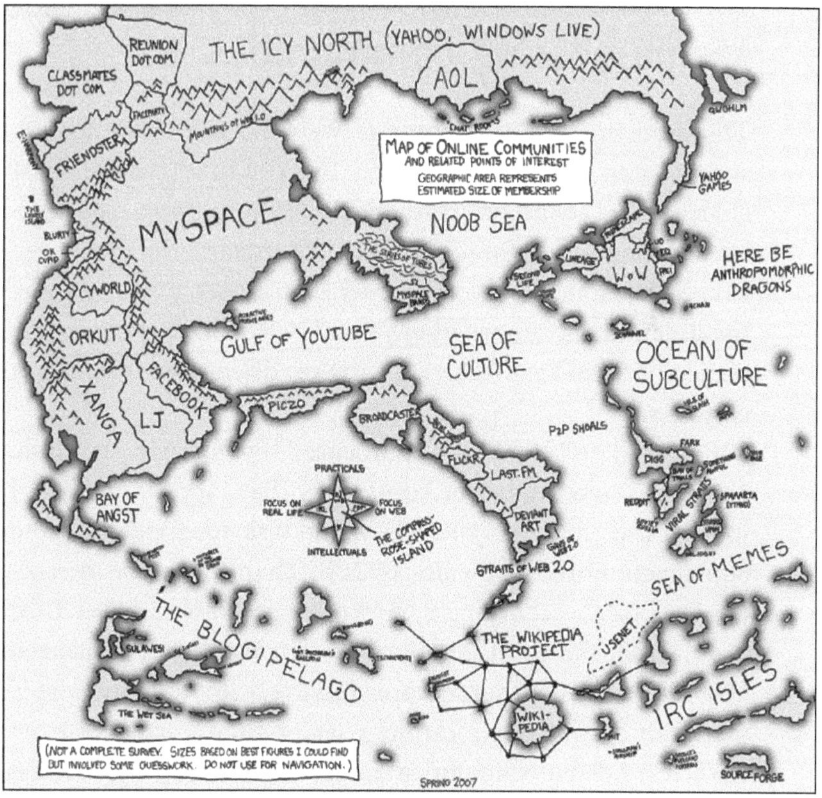

Source: http://xkcd.com/256/, courtesy of Randall Munroe

We're also starting to see signs of the next phase in the evolution of social networks. Vertical sites, such as LinkedIn.com with its focus on professional relationships, are gaining in popularity; this, like the rise of Facebook, is perhaps a reflection of the growing crossover between online and offline lives. The other trend, as the individual user's contribution to the internet becomes more and more scattered across the increasing range of neat social tools and technologies, is towards aggregator sites like FriendFeed, where people can track all of their friends' activities – their blog posts, their Flickr uploads, their Facebook status updates – via a single page.

Media-sharing communities

The other increasingly popular Web 2.0 site is the media-sharing community, as typified by YouTube (where users share video content) and Flickr (photograph sharing). Media-sharing communities generally make it as quick and easy as possible to upload content, and once it's on the site the user can choose whether to make it publicly available or restrict access to a select group of designated friends or contacts.

Founded in 2005 and purchased by Google in 2006, YouTube (www.youtube.com) now has approximately 4 million user channels and 84 million uploaded videos,[17] and consumed more bandwidth in 2007 than the entire internet did in 2000.[18] According to Alexa's traffic ranking, YouTube is currently the third most popular website on the internet. Not bad for a site that features relatively low-quality hosted video on a completely random set of topics, ranging from the latest hot-button political issues to the seemingly endless amount of fun that can be had incinerating marshmallow peeps in a microwave. But YouTube is like Wikipedia in that it's all about the connections: it's one of those sites where the joy of browsing is in the related videos that show up in the sidebar next to the one you went there to view. (I will confess at this point that my last visit to YouTube was to watch the thought-provoking video 'We think' that introduces Charles Leadbetter's latest book; half an hour later I found myself watching a video of someone's pet skunk attempting – unsuccessfully – to make his way down a flight of stairs.)

YouTube also includes easy-to-use sharing tools that make it simple to embed videos in your blog, webpage or MySpace profile, allowing popular videos to spread rapidly across the web, with many going viral in a relatively short space of time – as can be attested by the unwitting stars of some of YouTube's most popular videos, the Star Wars Kid (www.youtube.com/watch?v=HPPj6viIBmU, 9 million views) and the Numa Numa Guy (www.youtube.com/watch?v=60og9gwKh1o&feature=related, 17 million views). Fifty seconds of unintentional streaker footage at a soccer game in Vancouver netted the author 150,000 YouTube views (Figure 1.7).

Registered users can comment on videos uploaded by other users, or post their own videos in response. The general quality of dialogue on YouTube comment threads tends to be quite excruciating, but there is certainly no lack of it – and no lack of users keen to share their personal videos on the World Wide Web. At current estimates, approximately ten hours of video are uploaded to YouTube every minute.[19]

Perhaps unsurprisingly, copyright issues and offensive material are both significant issues for YouTube. It has been the subject of legal action by disgruntled entertainment companies,[20] and although it prohibits the uploading of

Figure 1.7 You too can have a viral video

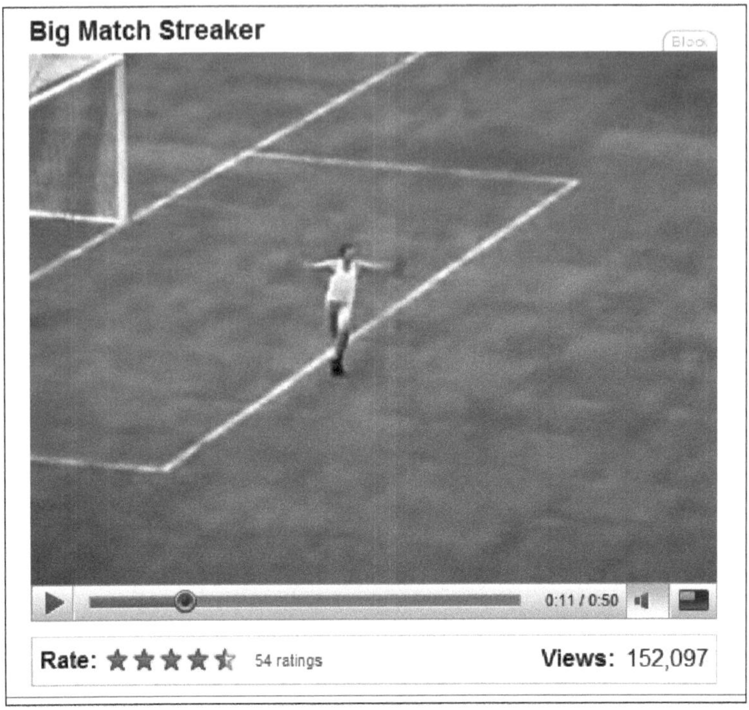

Source: www.youtube.com/watch?v=Y3uAXWeeKzo

illegal, offensive or pornographic material, there are no formal measures in place to ensure swift removal and the flagging of inappropriate content is left up to the community.

Photo-sharing site Flickr (www.flickr.com) is another of Web 2.0's greatest hits. Flickr was founded in 2004, and purchased by Google a year later. The site now hosts more than 2 billion photographs and estimates that between 3 million and 5 million new photographs are uploaded to the site every day.[21] Public photos are open for comments from other users, and can be made favorites by anyone who particularly likes that picture. Flickr also enables users to create groups where like-minded photographers can gather to share their pictures and comment on photos and photography techniques.

Flickr's free account is quite limited. Users can upload up to 100 MB of photos per month, and only the most recent 200 will display in their photostream. They are also limited to just three sets of pictures, and can only post to ten group pools. However, at just $25 per month for a Pro account that allows unlimited uploading and storage, cost is not a significant barrier to entry.

Flickr and YouTube are by no means unique as sharing communities – photo-sharing sites such as Fotki (www.fotki.com) and Photobucket (www.photobucket.com) offer similar services, and Vimeo (www.vimeo.com) offers video hosting at considerably better quality than YouTube – but they are excellent examples of sites where users can share personal content and then connect with one another to discuss and comment on it.

One of the most interesting things about Flickr, YouTube and similar sites is how willing people are to make this kind of personal content publicly available. Part of it is ease of use – it's much easier to send a link to the video of a family party to your not terribly tech-savvy grandmother if she doesn't have to register for a YouTube account in order to view it – but part of it is that, in the Web 2.0 environment, our notion of privacy is changing. While still wary of the threats that exist online, we're seeing a new value in sharing our photographs, videos and other content. This is very important for libraries, with their deep concern and legal obligations regarding user privacy.

Online library tools

The past couple of years have also seen a huge surge in the popularity of online library applications, like LibraryThing and Shelfari. These are essentially tools that allow users to catalogue and share their personal book collections online. LibraryThing launched in 2005, and currently boasts 26 million books and 34 million tags.[22] It draws data from Amazon, the Library of Congress and more than 80 other libraries that allow open access to their catalogues using the Z39.50 protocol. This enables registered users to organize their collections by Dewey or LoC classification. Users can also make their own subject tags to create an informal folksonomy with which to organize their collections.

Online library tools also act as social spaces for readers, enabling them to share their collections and rate and discuss books online. Shelfari has online book groups where users can gather and talk about their latest reads, and LibraryThing will flag libraries that are similar to yours and make recommendations 'based on the collective intelligence of other libraries'.[23] Authors are actively involved in these tools, with the opportunity to register as official authors and then use the platforms to engage and interact with their readers.

Adding a book to LibraryThing is very straightforward; you simply select the 'Add a Book' tab, check the appropriate boxes to let LibraryThing know if you would prefer to search the Library of Congress, Amazon, or both, and then click on the title when it appears in the search results to add it to your collection. Because it draws on such a wide range of data, LibraryThing even provides details and cover art for the various different editions of books. Tags and ratings can either be included when the title is selected or added afterwards using a 'Quick Edit' feature.

LibraryThing is very aware of its roots in the library world, and has also developed LibraryThing for Libraries – a paid product that integrates the social discovery elements of the website with library catalogues. LibraryThing for

Libraries allows libraries to include book recommendations, tag-based browsing and links to other editions and translations of individual works through the inclusion of a few lines of HTML in the existing iPac interface (Figure 1.8). It offers a very simple and effective way for libraries to enhance their catalogues without needing to worry about the difficulty of performing extensive back-end customizations.

There are some limitations to the application. It doesn't integrate with the ILS on the back end, so libraries are required to send either a list of ISBNs or a tab-delimited file containing the author, title and ISBN for all items that they want enhanced; and while the appearance of the interface is fully customizable, more significant troubleshooting at the content level has to be referred back to LibraryThing. Libraries don't have control over the algorithms that filter out inappropriate or unsuitable tags, or the ability to add their own tags to an iPac record. However, LibraryThing for Libraries is one of the very few ways to introduce simple social content into the library catalogue, and more than 50 libraries are currently using LibraryThing content in their iPacs.

Other Web 2.0 trends

Mash-ups

Mash-ups are used to describe the new products or services created when tech-savvy users combine the APIs and/or data from two or more sites into a new application or service. A great example of a useful mash-up is the Maplandia news site (www.maplandia.com/news). Maplandia's creators use the Google Maps API to present an interactive map of world

FIGURE 1.8 West Vancouver Memorial Library's WebPac catalogue, showing LibraryThing content ('Similar Books' and 'Tags')

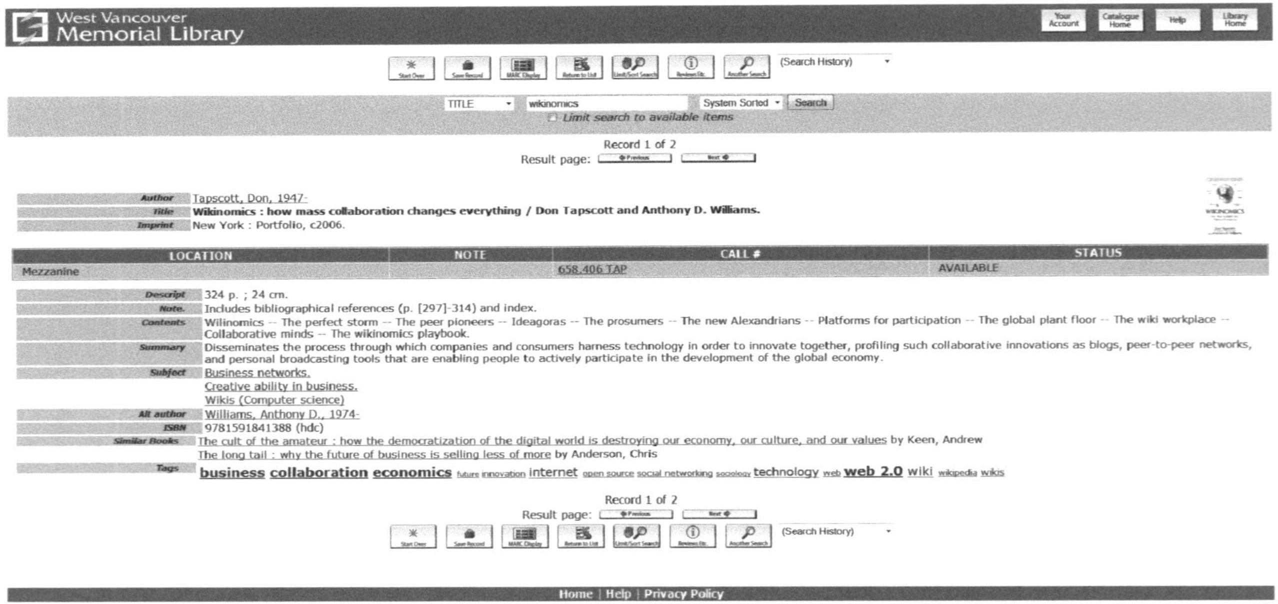

Source: http://catalogue.westvanlib.org/search/Xtitle:(wikinomics)&SORT=D/Xtitle:(wikinomics)&SORT=D&SUBKEY=title%3A(wikinomics)/1%2C2%2C2%2CB/frameset&FF=Xtitle:(wikinomics)&SORT=D&2%2C2%2C

news for any given day. News items are browsable by date; clicking on a date presents a world map where small markers indicate countries where significant news items happened on that day (Figure 1.9). Clicking the markers opens a call-out window showing the headlines, which also appear underneath the map with a series of flags showing other countries where that news item was reported.

In order to create the mash-up Maplandia's creators tagged news stories with geo-tags, enabling them to be

Figure 1.9 Maplandia world map

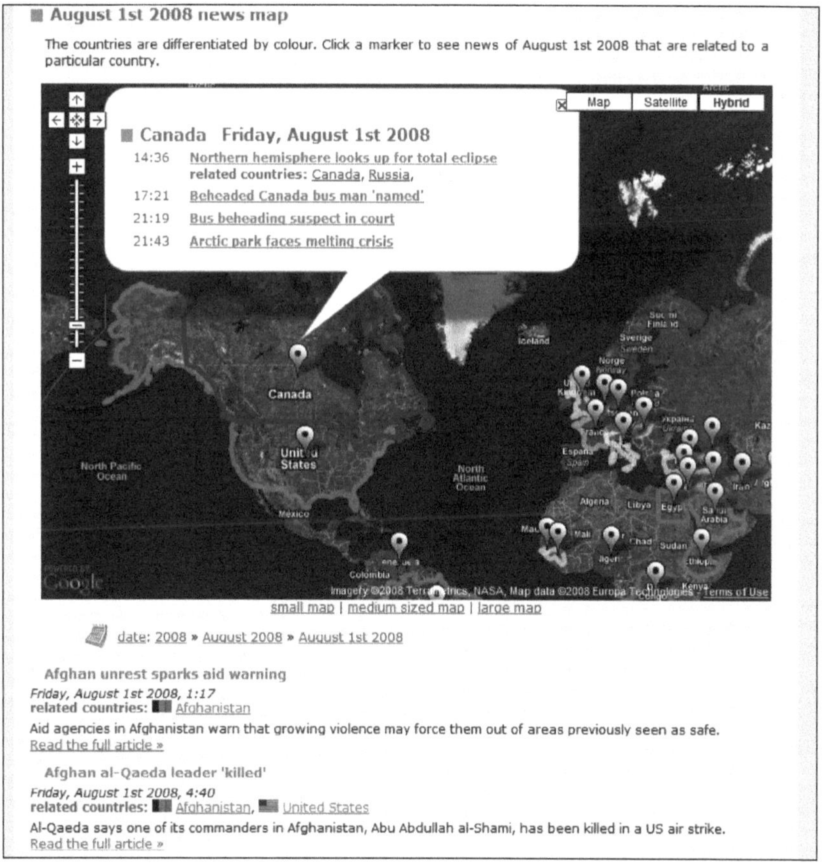

Source: www.maplandia.com/news/

connected with the locations on Google Maps where the stories took place. In addition to the world map, maps are available for North America, South America, Europe, Asia, Africa and Australia.

Another mash-up which has received significant media attention is EveryBlock (www.everyblock.org). EveryBlock started out as ChicagoCrime.org, which combined the Google Maps API and official crime data for the city of Chicago to allow users to see exactly how many muggings, auto thefts, murders and other criminal activities had been reported in specific neighborhoods and even individual streets. It has now evolved into EveryBlock, which aggregates local data from around the web to provide an online 'newspaper' for every city block in eight major US cities. EveryBlock crawls the web to collect and pool civic and government information, articles from both major and local newspapers and social content such as Flickr photographs, local business reviews and Craigslist postings; these can then be searched by news type, neighborhood, city block, map or timeline.

EveryBlock is a typical mash-up in that it uses data from multiple sources across the web, combining and repurposing them so that they are delivered in a form that's meaningful to users seeking information about their neighborhood. The whole philosophy of mash-ups is one of data that are fluid and reusable, easily repackaged into the format most helpful to the user. Not that long ago, the idea of such open APIs and free-and-easy development would have been anathema in a corporate world where such data were still considered proprietary and a closely guarded secret. Now, it's generally accepted that a more collaborative, open model, where APIs are opened to the vast wealth of talent, imagination and ideas out there on the net, is a far more rapid and productive way of achieving true innovation. And even if that innovation comes from outside the company that created the original product, if it helps put its product on the map then it's not necessarily a bad thing.

Widgets

Widgets are essentially small pieces of code that users can take and embed in their own websites to present information or perform a particular function. Many popular websites offer a range of widgets that users can embed in their sites to enhance their own offerings while simultaneously promoting the original site; there are also a number of sites dedicated to widget creation.

LibraryThing, for example, allows users to create widgets by asking them to select a few parameters (widget style, number of titles to display in the widget, tags and content details) and then turning this into a small piece of JavaScript code (Figure 1.10). The code can be used on a small scale by individual users to showcase their LibraryThing collections on their own websites, or on a much larger scale by libraries to profile their latest titles or specific areas of the collection. All that's required is that the titles are already entered in LibraryThing, which is a very straightforward process. The JavaScript is generated automatically, so no technical knowledge on the part of the user is required.

This is all well and good if you want to create a widget specific to an individual website or service. But a really great option for libraries looking to promote their own services is Widgetbox, a site that allows you to turn any Flash application, website, blog, RSS feed, Google Gadget or piece of HTML or JavaScript into a widget (Figure 1.11). It's literally as simple as pasting in the URL for the blog or website, clicking a button and then selecting from a handful

FIGURE 1.10 LibraryThing widget

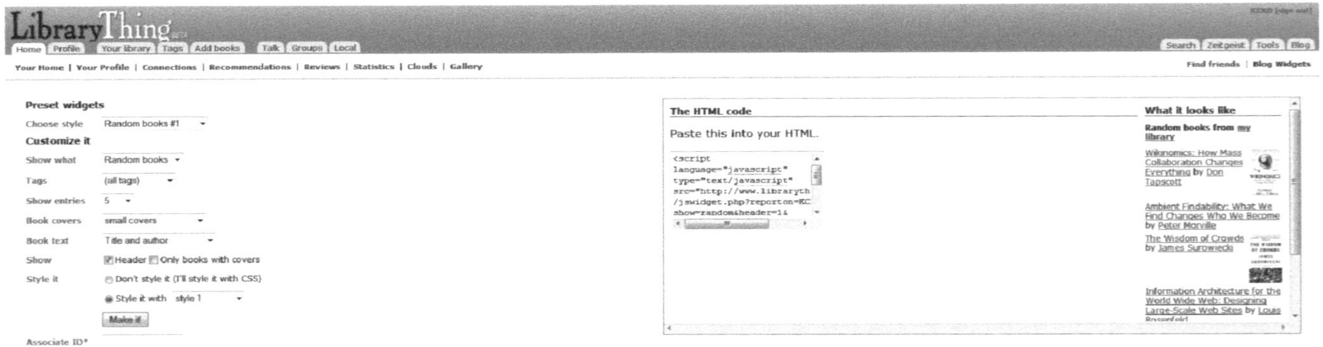

Source: www.librarything.com/widget

Figure 1.11 This widget uses one of VPL's RSS feeds to display newly added titles on the subject of citizenship and immigration

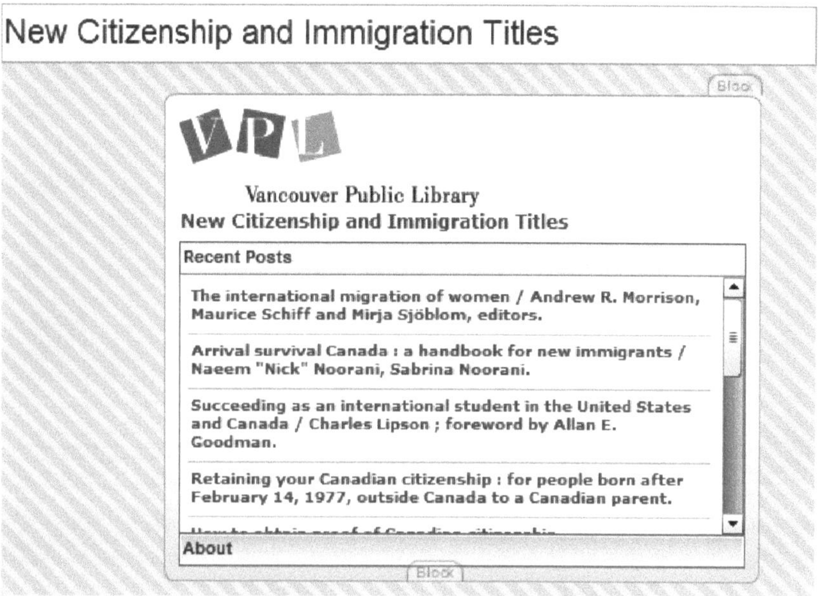

Source: www.widgetbox.com/widget/new-citizenship-and-immigration-titles

of customization options to choose the widget's appearance. These kinds of widgets can be used for improved delivery of existing content, and can also be made available to users to embed in their own webpages or blogs. This allows users to enhance their webpages with dynamic content while also acting as a promotional tool for the originating site.

Another popular use for widgets is to increase opportunities for live dialogue. Chat services such as Meebo offer chat widgets that can be embedded in individual webpages. These take the form of a box in which the user can type a question, which then appears as a new instant message in the account of the page owner provided they're logged on. QuestionPoint, one of the largest providers of chat reference software to libraries, recently launched the

Qwidget, which enables libraries that use QuestionPoint to embed an 'Ask for help' box in any page on their websites (Figure 1.12). Any questions that are entered are immediately placed in the QuestionPoint chat queue, just as though that patron had clicked on the 'Chat with us' button, opened a viewport and submitted the question in the traditional way. These chat widgets remove some of the steps that users typically have to go through to connect with live help, and because they can be located anywhere on the site they increase the usability and user-friendliness of the website significantly.

Figure 1.12 The QuestionPoint Qwidget in action at Arlington Heights Memorial Library

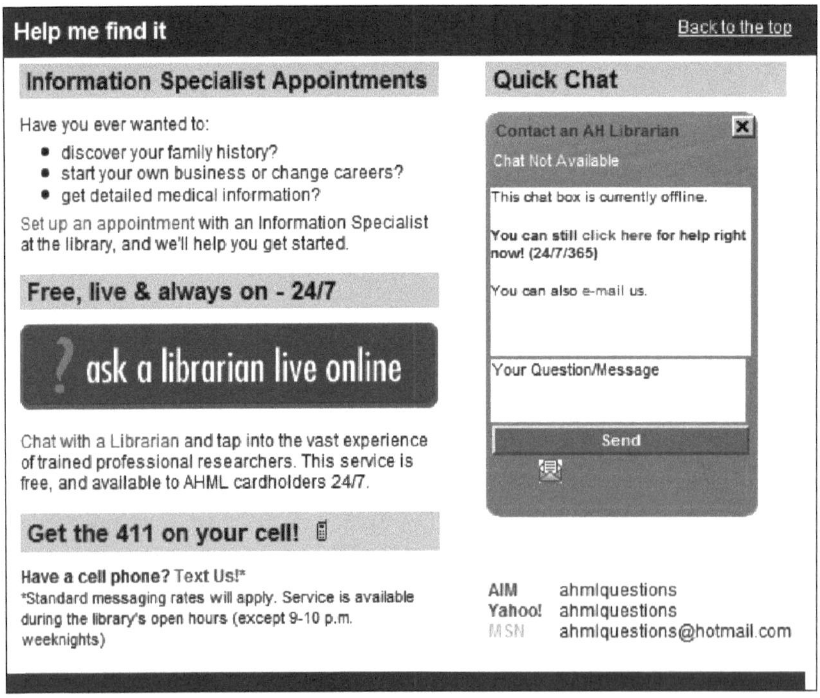

Source: www.ahml.info/find_information/

Folksonomies

Folksonomies are taxonomy-for-the-masses: user-defined, bottom-up classification systems that rely on open-ended tagging rather than a traditional, top-down classification hierarchy. The label 'folksonomy' was coined by information architect Thomas Vander Wal, and combines the terms 'folk' and 'taxonomy' to refer to these user-created content categorization systems.[24]

Folksonomies don't tend to exist independently, but rather develop from features incorporated into popular websites that allow users to classify and categorize the data collected in those sites. For example, Flickr allows users to tag their photographs; YouTube allows them to tag their videos; and LibraryThing allows them to tag their books. These tags can then be shared and searched, allowing users to find similar content and connect with people who share their interests.

Folksonomies are a great example of taking a traditional tool and seeing how it evolves when it's placed in the hands of the end user. Systems for classifying information are as old as the library profession itself, but folksonomies break away from the rigid constraints of Dewey classification or Library of Congress subject headings and allow users to create their own bottom-up organization, using the terminology that makes sense to them. The result is what Peter Morville has described as an immense increase in the overall findability of information.[25] The ideal folksonomy is a shared vocabulary of natural language terms that is accessible and meaningful to both new and existing users in the context in which it was created.

While these advantages are certainly significant, folksonomies are also somewhat anarchistic in their evolution and development, and suffer from the kind of drawbacks that are to be expected when the selection of classification language amounts to an intellectual free-for-all. With no set vocabulary, synonyms proliferate, as do stemming issues such as the inclusion of tags for both the singular and plural or active and passive versions of words. Incorrect or nonsensical tags are often included, as are tags by users who deliberately set out to be obscure, esoteric or overly descriptive with their tags. There is no fixed standard for multiple words, so whereas some sites concatenate others will treat the tag as two separate words. For example, applying the tag 'Galiano Island' to a set of photographs on one site might result in the tag being treated as 'GalianoIsland', whereas another site might separate the words and include the photograph not just with other pictures tagged with 'Galiano', but with all pictures tagged as 'Island'.

There are options for resolving some of the inaccuracies in existing folksonomies. For example, LibraryThing filters out unique or rarely used tags when supplying social data to library catalogues through LibraryThing for Libraries; this decreases the chances of highly personal tags that are used only by specific individuals making it through to the iPacs. Some sites also review content and apply standardized terminology to it before making it a permanent part of the collection or knowledge base; others review and edit user-created terminology to ensure a degree of consistency.

In spite of these difficulties, tagging remains a hugely popular activity on the internet. Tags are incorporated into almost every kind of user-generated content, from photographs to videos and blog posts. There is a lot that libraries can learn by comparing folksonomies to terms from our traditional taxonomies, like Library of Congress subject headings. How do they compare? What kinds of information do we find when we browse tags rather than searching subject headings? Are there obvious demarcations in the way users identify information as compared to the fixed terminology that we use?

Multimedia content enhancement

New web applications are also creating opportunities to enhance static content and turn it into a full multimedia experience. A simple screen-capture tool like Jing (www.jingproject.com) can be used to create a step-by-step 'how to' guide to show users the different resources available on the library's website, or to introduce them to a new subscription database. Study guides no longer have to be static text; they can incorporate video, screen capture or even rich links to content elsewhere on the web. Apture, for example, is a really neat tool that allows users to add a mouseover snapshot to any hyperlink on their webpages (Figure 1.13). This can display text excerpts, photographs and even video clips from the sites being linked to, turning flat text into a rich multimedia experience and bringing a webpage alive.

Enter the semantic web

But are we really still in the Web 2.0 phase? A zero phase suggests a brand-new product, one for the early adopters. The current web model has moved somewhat beyond that; the read/write web with its plethora of wiki technologies, blogging platforms and social networking sites has been around for a few years now. The straightforward social networking sites that characterized the initial push towards 2.0 – Facebook, Twitter et al. – are starting to be superseded

Figure 1.13 Apture-enhanced article: mouseover the artist's name to hear one of his songs

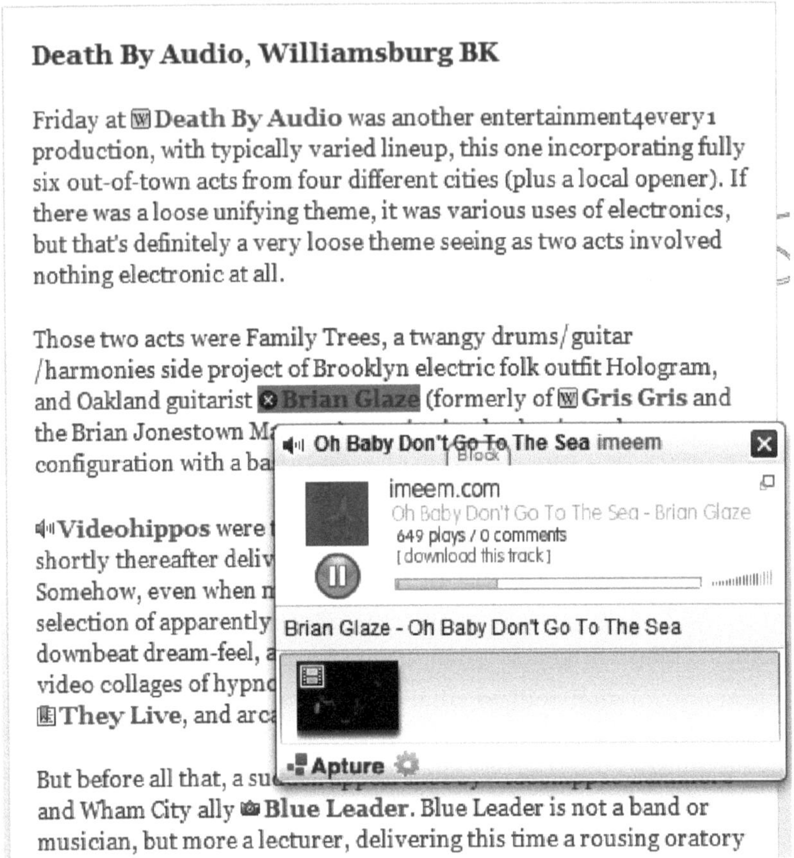

Source: www.apture.com/experience/

by aggregator sites like FriendFeed and Swurl, where content from all the various communities to which a member belongs is gathered together and presented in one place. This suggests that, at the very least, we've reached 2.1.

In fact, web technologies are rapidly reaching 3.0: the semantic web. If Web 2.0 is about people increasingly using the web to collaborate, share and converse, Web 3.0 is about having computers do the hard work of finding the conversations that we actually want to be involved in and the projects in which we'd like to participate. It's about using common standards to build a framework where machines can understand web content without human direction.

For libraries, a key part of remaining relevant since the rise of the internet has been the extra value we bring to search results. Google might be able to return 14 million hits on your keyword search, and its PageRank algorithms can give you a rough idea of which ones are the most useful, but it can't pin down the true authority and relevance of a given source the way a librarian can. A key question that the emergence of semantic web technologies raises for librarians is that if these technologies can become truly effective and mainstream, how much of the value that traditionally only humans have been able to bring to information retrieval will semantic search tools be able to add?

Most semantic web applications are still in beta, but many of them are already generating significant interest from the big players. Powerset (www.powerset.com/), the first semantic search engine, was recently acquired by Microsoft amid rumors that a marriage of the two could result in the first real 'Google-killer' search engine. Powerset uses natural phrasing rather than keywords to search, and highlights relevant terms in its results page – so a search that asks 'Who did Henry VIII marry?' will return not only the details, but have the names of his wives highlighted in yellow.[26] This is not dissimilar to the most basic value-add of a public library's virtual reference service, where the librarian uses chat software to push pages to patrons and direct them to the sections that contain the information they need.

Twine (www.twine.com) is one of the most advanced semantic websites currently available, and for those lucky enough to get in on the beta test it's certainly looking very promising. Users weave websites, articles, notes, photographs and videos together in topic-specific threads called Twines, tagging as they go. Twine then uses semantic language processing to identify Twines and other Twinerians (Twine creators) that users may like, based on their current interests and posted items. Its language-processing algorithms are also smart enough to search through the tags and identify ones that fall into specific categories: places, companies, people (Figure 1.14).

Having been part of the Twine beta test for some time now, I've been extremely impressed by how little dross has hit my screen. Although this may be in part due to the fact that Twine is still a gated community – at the time of writing, the site has approximately 30,000 beta testers registered – a bit of digging shows me that there's plenty of content on Twine that I'm not interested in. But Twine has figured out that I'm not interested, and isn't showing it to me. That's pretty impressive. It will be very interesting to see how the site develops once it opens its doors to the world, and how libraries will respond if there are websites out there that can not only respond to natural language search terms, but can automatically organize and present information in a meaningful way.

The future is now

What we are seeing at the moment is the emergence of a new information environment. In this new environment, the end-users' relationship with information – and their perception of that relationship – has changed. Children are now

FIGURE 1.14 Twine: semantic discovery

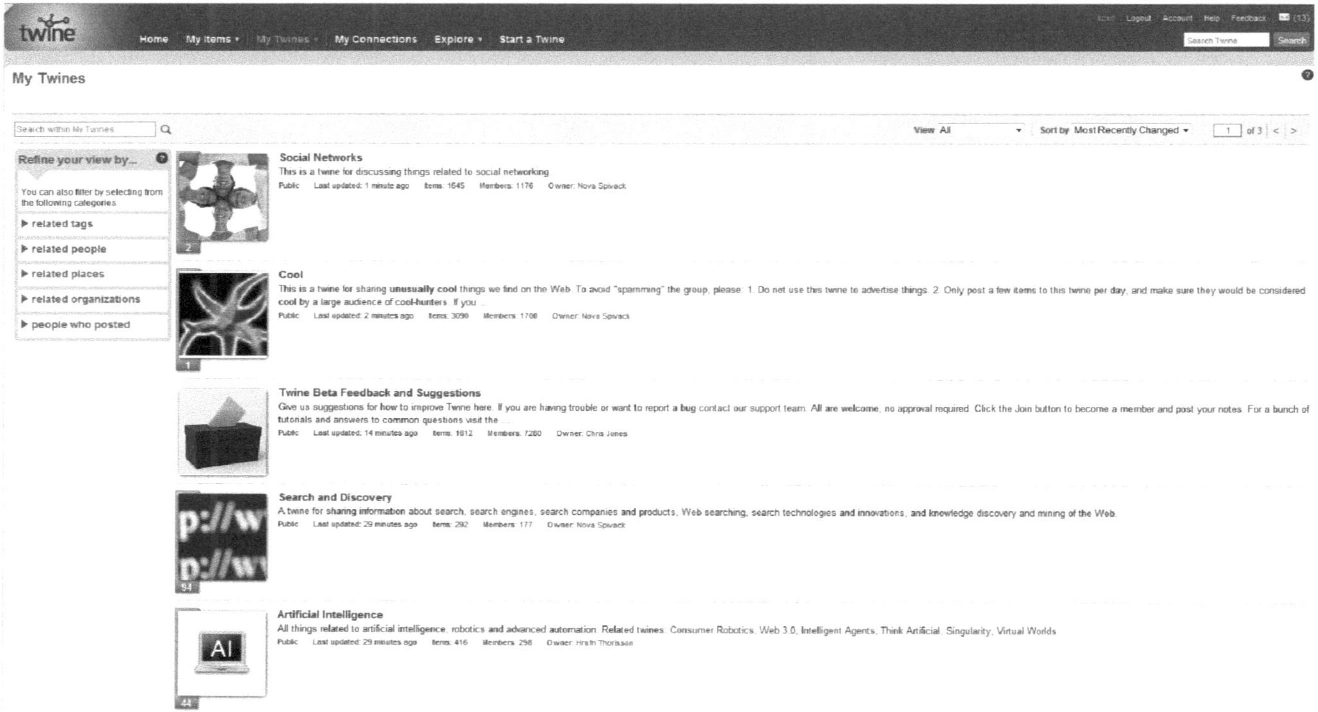

Source: www.twine.com/twines

growing up in a world where they take it as read that any fact they need to find out will be available at the touch of a button, or as many buttons as it takes to type that keyword into a search engine. The internet has been around for long enough that even those of us who didn't grow up with the net accept it as a completely ubiquitous presence, something we cannot imagine the world without. People's basic awareness of information – of the fact that it's out there, and that they *should* be able to find it – has never been greater.

In addition to an increased awareness of the amount and accessibility of information that's out there, the vast array of tools on offer on the modern web mean that users are able to exercise a significant degree of control over the way they search for and retrieve information. In a world dominated by the quick-and-dirty keyword search and the simplicity of Google's white space, a library catalogue interface is complex, inflexible and unfriendly. Users aren't used to the precision of subject headings and MARC records. These things are librarians' tools. In the old world, where there were no other options for tracking down relevant information, users accepted that they either needed to learn how to use these tools or had to ask an information professional to carry out the search for them. Now, users are defining their own tools of choice and growing increasingly frustrated with legacy applications like the traditional iPac.

As well as searchers, in this brave new environment everyone is – or can be – an author. Whether it's posting comments to a CBC news story, blogging about a topic that interests you or using Twitter to share brief glimpses into your life with friends and family, anyone with access to a computer and an internet connection can publish their thoughts and opinions on the web. End users no longer see themselves as passive absorbers of the information they need, but as creators and shapers of that information. Web

2.0 – the read/write web – has had a profound effect upon the way individuals react to and interact with information.

These changing relationships and perspectives have significant implications for libraries. We need to find a way to continue offering value to our users, to provide better answers than the automated tools. We also need to embrace the fact that our users no longer expect to sit back and take in information, but play an active role in creating it, sharing it and engaging in dialogue around it.

This is where we can take the Web 2.0 tools and technologies that have driven these trends and use them to our own advantage. Blogs offer us the chance to communicate directly with our users, providing regular updates and allowing them to respond with their feedback and thoughts. Wikis create an opportunity to embrace the expertise that exists in our communities, opening up our study guides for adaptation and refinement by experts in the disciplines that those guides cover. Discussion boards allow us to create virtual book clubs online. Multimedia content allows us to create online tutorials and guides, provide podcasts of popular author readings and share video of popular library events. Some libraries have been quick to embrace these new technologies, and are already offering some or all of the examples listed above. Other libraries are wary of this new model where much of the content is coming from our users, where the audience have as strong a voice as the author: after all, it challenges our basic understanding that when it comes to information, we're the experts.

If the world of Web 2.0 is a whole new environment for libraries, Web 3.0 promises even more rapidly shifting sands underfoot. Technology is changing so rapidly that it's impossible to second-guess what the killer app might be a year from now, never mind in five years' time. This is one of the things that make strategic planning for virtual library services so uniquely challenging: it's about being able to respond fast enough to take advantage of the trends without wasting a lot of time climbing on every passing bandwagon, and being able to remain relevant in an environment where we can't predict exactly what the future might hold.

Regardless of the technology, one thing we can guarantee is that only our users can tell us what we need to do to remain relevant to them. And that's where Web 2.0 gives us a vital edge: it offers an opportunity to engage our users in the virtual environment, to extend our interactions with them into this space and allow them to direct and guide the next stage of our evolution. Our task is to accept that we must surrender some control to our community, and then develop the tools that will allow them to provide us with meaningful input and enable us to make use of that knowledge.

Notes

1 Cited in Tomei, Lawrence (2008) *Encyclopedia of Information Technology Curriculum Integration*. Hershey: Idea Group Inc.
2 Meattle, James (2007) 'Top 50 websites ranked by unique visitors', *Compete*; available at: *http://blog.compete.com/2007/10/30/top-50-websites-domains-digg-youtube-flickr-facebook/* (accessed: 3 August 2008).
3 WordPress.com (2008) 'Homepage'; available at: *http://wordpress.com/* (accessed: 3 August 2008).
4 Sifry, Dave (2007) 'The state of the live web, April 2007', *Technorati*; available at: *http://technorati.com/weblog/2007/04/328.html* (accessed: 3 August 2008).
5 Tapscott, Don and Williams, Anthony D. (2006) *Wikinomics: How Mass Collaboration Changes Everything*. New York: Penguin.

6 Wikipedia (2008) 'Wikipedia'; available at: *http://en.wikipedia.org/wiki/Wikipedia* (accessed: 3 August 2008).
7 Wikipedia (2008) 'What Wikipedia is not'; available at: *http://en.wikipedia.org/wiki/Wikipedia:What_Wikipedia_is_not* (accessed: 3 August 2008).
8 Giles, Jim (2005) 'Internet encyclopedias go head to head', *Nature*, 438: 900–1.
9 Wikipedia, note 6 above.
10 Schwartz, Barry (2006) 'Yahoo! Answers birthday: one year old', *SearchEngineLand*, 13 December; available at: *http://searchengineland.com/061213-085832.php* (accessed: 3 August 2008).
11 Jasra, Manoj (2008) 'Yahoo! Answers ahead in Q&A site visits', *WebProNews*, 20 March; available at: *www.webpronews.com/blogtalk/2008/03/20/Yahoo!-answers-leads-the-way-in-qa-site-visits* (accessed: 3 August 2008).
12 Sellers, Patricia (2006) 'MySpace cowboys', *CNN*, 29 August; available at: *http://money.cnn.com/magazines/fortune/fortune_archive/2006/09/04/8384727/index.htm* (accessed: 3 August 2008).
13 Tynan, Dan (2006) 'The 25 worst websites', *PC World*, 15 September; available at: *www.pcworld.com/article/127116-7/the_25_worst_web_sites.html* (accessed: 3 August 2008).
14 Alexa (2008) 'Myspace.com traffic details'; available at: *www.alexa.com/data/details/traffic_details/myspace.com* (accessed: 3 August 2008); Alexa (2008) 'Facebook traffic details'; available at: *www.alexa.com/data/details/ traffic_details/facebook.com* (accessed: 3 August 2008).
15 Facebook (2008) 'Statistics'; available at: *www.new.facebook.com/press/info.php?statistics* (accessed: 3 August 2008).
16 Greene, Jaye (2007) 'Microsoft and Facebook hook up', *BusinessWeek*, 25 October; available at: *www.businessweek.com/technology/content/oct2007/tc20071024_654439.htm?chan=top+news_top+news+index_top+story* (accessed: 3 August 2008).
17 Alexa (2008) 'YouTube traffic details'; available at: *www.alexa.com/data/details/traffic_details/youtube.com* (accessed: 3 August 2008).

18 YouTube (2008) 'Search query*'; available at: *www.youtube.com/results?search_query=** (accessed: 3 August 2008).

19 Carter, Lewis (2008) 'Web could collapse as video demand soars', *Telegraph.co.uk*, 9 April; available at: *www.telegraph.co.uk/news/uknews/1584230/Web-could-collapse-as-video-demand-soars.html* (accessed: 3 August 2008).

20 *Telegraph.co.uk* (2008) 'YouTube lawsuit threatens internet freedom, claims Google', *Telegraph.co.uk*, 27 May; available at: *www.telegraph.co.uk/connected/main.jhtml?xml=/connected/2008/05/27/dlgoog127.xml* (accessed: 3 August 2008).

21 Arrington, Michael (2007) '2 billion photos on Flickr', *TechCrunch*, 13 November; available at: *www.techcrunch.com/2007/11/13/2-billion-photos-on-flickr/* (accessed: 3 August 2008).

22 LibraryThing (undated) 'FAQs: general'; available at: *www.librarything.com/forlibraries/about* (accessed: 3 August 2008).

23 LibraryThing (undated) 'About LibraryThing'; available at: *www.librarything.com/about* (accessed: 3 August 2008).

24 Mathes, Adam (2004) 'Folksonomies: cooperative classification and communication through shared metadata', Adammathes.com, December; available at: *www.adammathes.com/academic/computer-mediated-communication/folksonomies.html* (accessed: 3 August 2008).

25 Morville, Peter (2005) *Ambient Findability*. Sebastopol: O'Reilly Media.

26 Kopytoff, Verne (2008) 'Powerset ready for the prime time', *San Francisco Chronicle*, 11 May; available at: *www.sfgate.com/cgi-bin/article.cgi?f=/c/a/2008/05/11/BU1M10K06D.DTL* (accessed: 3 August 2008).

2

A dialogue, not a lecture: libraries as online communities

Web 2.0 has provided users with an enormous number of tools for creating content and making their voices heard in the online space. If libraries choose to embrace this content – as many are already doing – there is certainly no shortage of options out there. However, the question remains: why would we, as the information experts, invite user-generated content into our web spaces?

It's all about the user

One of the greatest challenges for public libraries in particular is how to remain relevant in an age when more information than anyone could ever process in a lifetime is just the touch of a button away. The traditional role of the library as guardian of information as a physical thing is gone, washed away by the storm-force tides of the web. We're reinventing ourselves in an age when the expectation is that information is not only free of charge but freely accessible. Instead of gatekeepers we're becoming guides, helping users separate the wheat from the chaff and find their way amid the sticky morass of fact and fiction that swirl together, often indistinguishably, on the web. This process of reinvention is a tricky one, particularly for a profession that has traditionally been unused to change and slow to respond to it.

No matter where we find ourselves at the end of this process, the one thing we must achieve to ensure that we not only survive but thrive in the new information age is to remain relevant to our users. The trouble is that when the sand is shifting so quickly underfoot, and the future rushing towards us so fast that it's impossible to focus on it long enough to make a clear prediction of what it holds, it's very hard to know what *relevant* is. The best way to find out is to allow the only people who know for sure – our users –to guide us.

Public libraries exist to serve patrons. Our mantra hasn't changed: *it's all about the user*. Whether creating new services, developing a program or ordering new materials, this should always be first and foremost in the librarian's mind. For us to remain relevant to our users, we need to understand what their expectations are. What do they need a public library to be in the new information environment? Should our focus remain on our traditional core services, our collections and reference desks? Or should we be exploring our role as a community space, offering a platform to writers and artists and hosting displays and programs? Should we reinvent ourselves as instructors and teachers, guiding people through the maze of the modern internet and ensuring that children grow up with the information literacy skills they need to understand truly the value of individual pieces of information? The possibilities are endless, and choosing between them is a challenge. We can't second-guess our patrons on this; we have to be sure that we're delivering what they want, and not what we think they want.

This is where Web 2.0 tools and software can give us a huge advantage. By inviting our patrons to begin contributing content, to add their voices to our websites – or going out on to the web to meet them in external web spaces, like Facebook pages or MySpace profiles – we're also inviting them to define what they want their libraries to be about. User engagement is the single best tool libraries have to ensure that we're going in the right direction and giving users what they really want rather than what we think they want. Providing patrons with a voice, and a platform from which they can make that voice heard, is the first step to allowing them a meaningful role in the planning and development of library services.

Canada's Working Together project is one of the leading advocates of handing control over to the community and allowing them to guide the evolution of library services and policies. In the *Community-Led Libraries Toolkit*, national coordinator Annette DeFaveri states:

> Involving community members in evaluating a planning process, service or policy ensures that the community *identifies what is relevant to them*. It also offers library staff the opportunity to truly see the library and its processes and services through the eyes of the users.[1]

Of course, this is not without its challenges. In our interactions with patrons we're used to thinking of ourselves as the experts. After all, we have the time in library school and the letters after our names to prove it. Being a librarian is, in many ways, all about control: strict sets of rules, consistently applied, that allow us to organize information and retrieve it when needed. Not only surrendering our control but accepting that when it comes to understanding the needs of the community we aren't necessarily the experts runs counter to the very nature of the profession – and yet it's only by doing this that we can truly succeed as librarians.

> The Community-Led Service Planning Model advocates for an important paradigm shift in library planning. In this model, librarians spend a significant amount of time learning from and working with the community. This model repositions library staff as learners and facilitators rather than experts.[2]

In a community-led planning model, typically the process would be for a library staff member to go out into the community, establish partnerships with community groups and then use these to build relationships with the individual community members. Once these relationships are established, the groups and individual members are prepared to have open and honest discussions with the librarian about what they would like to see their local library offer. This kind of engaged, progressive dialogue often results in profound changes in understanding about the existing barriers to library service and how they can be overcome. For example, poor attendance at a storytime might result not from lack of interest or unpopular themes, but from the fact that the library has failed to take into account the public transport schedule and thus made it difficult for parents without their own cars to reach the session.[3]

The online space offers an entirely different, but nonetheless important, way of engaging library users and increasing their involvement in service planning. Admittedly it would be hard to follow the typical community-led planning model online: community groups, for example, don't necessarily have their own online spaces that would replicate the function of a clubhouse or community center in the physical world. However, the social networking spaces of Facebook, MySpace, Twitter and LiveJournal do represent community gathering places of a different kind, and ones that offer just as much potential for libraries to engage their users in active, meaningful dialogue.

One of the interesting things about online space is that it may not necessarily require anything like the level of relationship building that is required in the offline world. Generally, the folk who spent their time on social networking sites, who post and share information publicly and engage in discussion and dialogue, are more than willing to participate in online conversations. And in the virtual space, feedback is immediate and emotive. Users are honest – sometimes brutally so – especially when they have the reassurance of relative anonymity.

There are many ways we can use current web tools to encourage users to enter into dialogue about the library. We can approach them directly with a survey or discussion topic, asking what they want to see in a library and what their priorities for library services are, and follow up on their responses in a way that's not possible with traditional survey tools. We can introduce blogs on our own websites allowing people to comment on library programs and events that they've attended, and use the responses to gauge the success of those programs. Or we can go into external web spaces and build Facebook pages and MySpace profiles, and use these to encourage debate and dialogue away from the library's own web presence. The results will often be unpredictable, but on the modern web the one guarantee is that there will be no shortage of voices. The platforms have already been built, and people have come in droves. What we must do is devise the methodologies by which we can take advantage of this to gain the feedback we need to inform the development of meaningful services.

Creating community spaces

The traditional library website is, when compared to the standards of the modern web, a lecture rather than a dialogue; a walled garden rather than an open space; a collection rather than a branch. We have typically treated our websites as online extensions of the physical collections that exist in our buildings. We use them to offer newspaper articles, journal articles, indexes, research guides and booklists: the typical tools of our trade. By opening up our websites to user-generated content – by inviting our users into the walled garden – we have the potential to turn our websites from collections into virtual branches: living, evolving spaces where people come together and interact.

The medium of choice

Inviting user-generated content on to our sites also turns them into the kind of spaces that our users are increasingly expecting and looking for online. Universal McCann's 2008 'Media in Mind' study found that more than 50 per cent of all US adults now use some form of social media for communication, with 10 per cent of adults publishing their own blogs. Among the 18–34 age group the figures are even higher: 85 per cent use social media as their main means of communication, and 20 per cent publish blogs.[4] A recent survey conducted by the RSA in the UK found that 56 per cent of respondents thought that 'online collaboration and deliberate participation will become the dominant method by which we organize ourselves'.[5]

Traditionally, libraries have expected their patrons to learn to use their tools of choice to search for and retrieve information. The Dewey Decimal System, while bringing order to chaos, is very much a librarian's tool that the unfamiliar patron often struggles to negotiate. In a generation more used to the broad subject headings and browsability of physical and online bookstores, Dewey generally only makes sense to people who have had time to learn how the system works and appreciate the value of its very precise organization.

The library catalogue is another legacy application that often creates a barrier to accessing information and resources. In the world of the keyword search, where Google is still the beacon that lights the way for most, a system organized around authority headings and precise subject terms provides unexpected, frustrating results to untrained users. The majority of library patrons simply don't think in these terms, and the more dominant keyword and natural-language search becomes, the less sense it will make to them. Most iPacs fail to provide anything like the relevance of a PageRank results list in response to their keyword search options, leading to even greater frustration.

The evolution of the ILS and the patron-facing iPac has been very much dominated by a handful of companies, restricting the opportunities for true innovation and change. Although some libraries have begun experimenting with tools like LibraryThing to enter social data into their existing catalogues, most iPacs remain little more than glorified card catalogues ported online. On the social web, our users are used to participating in conversations. The library catalogue gives them a lecture, and moreover uses jargon that they don't understand as it does so.

Library users also don't understand (quite reasonably) the very significant fact that the library catalogue and the library website are two separate pieces of infrastructure, and the operational consequences of this separation. A 2007 Vancouver Public Library patron survey revealed enormous frustration over the two separate login procedures required to access My Account functionality in the catalogue and access subscription electronic resources on the website. The two logins were seen as unnecessary, time-consuming and needlessly complex, especially as they require the exact same information to be repeated both times. Users consistently requested a single login, preferably with a user-selected login name and password rather than the full library barcode and PIN.[6] There was no indication that any users understood that these two items offered at www.vpl.ca might be fundamentally separate, and the dual logins a necessity – and why would they? The more seamless the wider web grows, with increasing uptake of applications like OpenID (which creates a single digital identity that can then be used to authenticate a user on multiple sites), the more these legacy frustrations will create barriers to access for our users.

As social networking software and other participatory web technologies bring more and more of people's lives online, they enable users to identify the tools that work for them. Even the broadest web trends provide us with valuable information about the tools that make the most sense and are easiest for people to use. The best example of this is perhaps the most obvious of all: Google. A bit-player on a scene dominated by AltaVista and Yahoo! when it first emerged, its incredibly rapid rise and subsequent unchallenged dominance of the online search world reveals much about what people are looking for in any search appliance. They value simplicity over complexity; keywords over Boolean searches; ease of use over precision; and most of all, they value relevant results.

The current popularity of tools and services that allow users to participate actively in communities is sending us an important message about what is required to ensure that patrons engage in a library website. Social networking, online communication and participatory content generation are no longer optional extras: they're expected. So expected, in fact, that two of the most popular self-publishing platforms currently used for blogging – WordPress and Moveable Type – have recently announced that their latest releases will include tools that allow people to add discussion forums, member profiles, friends lists and content rating abilities to their WordPress or MT-based blog or website.

> With both of the big players extending their traditional blogging platforms to offer social networking features, you have to wonder if traditional blogging is on its way out. For many years, web pundits have been saying that social networking would gain in popularity to such an extent that it would become a feature, not a destination in and of itself. These latest designs from MT and WordPress seem to prove that point.[7]

While it's unlikely that an individual blogger's social network will expand to the point where it would be able to rival Facebook or MySpace, this announcement is further proof of how ubiquitous social networking features have become on the web. Five years ago the novelty was in the ease with which the web allowed everyone to become an author, and share their opinions and expertise with the world. Now, if there's no option to discuss those opinions, to rate, challenge and explore them, interest flags rapidly. If libraries don't recognize this, and fail to offer opportunities for user dialogue, our websites will be left behind: static spaces that have failed to evolve and meet our users' expectations.

Embracing the intelligence of the masses

User-generated content allows us to explore the intelligence of the masses, the expertise that exists in our communities. Imagine, for example, a library-created study guide on child health. Diligently researched by the librarian, on a traditional site the guide is the product of one or perhaps two people. It offers a list of great titles on the topic, linking to those titles in the library catalogue. It offers the names of the best subscription databases on the topic, and suggested keyword searches to retrieve the most relevant articles. It even provides a set of carefully chosen links to the best external websites on the topic, hand-picked and annotated by the librarian. It's a great study guide, comprehensive and helpful. But it's static; read-only.

Now imagine turning that guide into a wiki, where any user can add to or edit the content. A pediatrician browsing the library website finds the guide and adds a section to it including links to the websites that he finds most helpful in the course of his work, and a brief synopsis of key information based on his own knowledge and experience. A mom of four in a low-income area adds another section with links to local organizations that provided her with helpful advice and support when one of her children was seriously ill. And another user comments with a completely different yet still relevant set of experiences, and another and another – and suddenly you have a guide that gathers in expertise from all kinds of different sources and perspectives. This read/write guide brings in experience, expertise and knowledge that extend far beyond the library walls. Users are empowered to create their own content, sharing it in a space that gives it credibility and value, and the library embraces the collective knowledge of the community to create highly relevant, comprehensive information products.

A wider reach

By incorporating existing technologies, tools and social networks into your virtual services, you can reach far larger audiences than you might reach through your website alone. In 2004 Vancouver Public Library surveyed users of its virtual reference services, Find It Now and Homework Help, and found that 21 per cent of respondents had never visited a VPL branch or contacted the library via telephone.[8] Yet these same users were returning night after night to seek help with their homework questions and work projects using the live chat service. Find It Now and Homework Help were quite literally accessing an entirely new pool of library users, showing them the value of library-assisted search and providing the same benefits to users as a face-to-face interaction at the reference desk.

When the Virtual Library, which managed the service, probed a little deeper, it identified certain trends among previous non-users of the library who were using the live chat service. There was a core contingent of ESL users for whom English is a second language and who found that virtual reference enabled them to take advantage of live service while also providing the benefit of written text that they had time to digest and understand, without the immediate pressures of a telephone conversation. Children in the K–12 age group whose parents had never taken them to the library, but who had learned about the service through their schools or peers, were another core group.[9]

Inviting conversation on to our websites, and embracing the tools that allow us to do so, is another method of engaging with users who might never have previously entered the library. For example, a problem that libraries often face with their book clubs is over-registration. The book club ends up with a wait list, and frustrated patrons who were looking forward to participating get turned away at the reference desk. If the library has an online book club to offer as an alternative, managed perhaps through a PHP bulletin board or other discussion tool, there are no limits to the number of users who can register. Rather than turning people away from the desk, the library can offer them a viable alternative which might not have the immediate social interaction of a face-to-face book-club meeting, but brings other benefits to compensate.

With a virtual book club there's no requirement to be at a certain place at a certain time: participants can join in the discussion as and when they are able. Users who might be excluded from the regular book club because of physical limitations – for example, home-bound outreach users who are not able to get to the library for a meeting – can participate freely. There are no limits on membership, so the club can easily accommodate all interested patrons and expand far beyond the branch, drawing in a wider range of points of view than would be possible in a traditional book club and making for a more lively and wide-ranging discussion.

Libraries are finally learning to step outside their own web spaces and establish a presence on social networking sites like Facebook, MySpace and Twitter. By creating profiles and promoting events and services on these sites, a library can reach users who have perhaps never entered the physical building and have no idea what services the library might be able to offer them.

Scalability

One of the great things about Web 2.0 is that it offers an application for every library, regardless of size or expertise. If a particular library doesn't have the expert knowledge or the staff time to create or customize an application, there's generally a solution out there that can be used to achieve the desired result. For example, if the software that powers your library's website doesn't have the capacity to add a blog to the site, starting a WordPress blog is very quick and easy – you just sign up for an account, and then use the intuitive dashboard to manage your blog posts. A number of pre-set designs allow you to customize the look and feel of the blog, although full customization so that it matches the style of your own website requires the addition of custom CSS and is a little more complex. The blog's URL, which generally takes the form of http://mylibrary.wordpress.com, can easily be redirected to any domain owned by the library, resulting in seamless user navigation.

Widgets are even easier to add; as discussed in the previous chapter, they usually require little more than the URL of your website or blog to get started. The site producing the widget then does all the work for you. One of the simplest and most effective widget installs is LibraryThing: this allows you to take your weekly or monthly new titles list, enter it into your LibraryThing library, and then use the LibraryThing application to produce a snippet of JavaScript code that you can embed into the front page of your site to present the new titles in an attractive, interactive manner for your users.

Starting a Twitter account is another very easy way of establishing new connections with your users. All you need to get started are a user name and password; updates can be any content that can be handily summarized in 140 characters or less (the length of a Twitter microblog post). Library events, news updates and even new titles can be presented in a Twitter feed. Twitter widgets also allow you to embed your feed into your existing website, or you can encourage your users to find you on Twitter and follow your updates there.

These are just a handful of examples, and we'll look in more detail at how these are set up and what libraries are doing with these kinds of applications later in the book. The important thing is that with Web 2.0 tools you don't have to be a programming expert or developer to take advantage. You can start small and then build up, or you may find that small is all you need when it comes to your own library's capacity.

Forces of change

User-generated content is a vital part of turning a library into a true community. It enables us to learn more about our patrons and what they want from their library; it enables us to facilitate and record conversation and interaction, in keeping with our role as custodians of the community memory; it enables us to access new pools of knowledge and expertise that exist outside of the library's walls.

It also means that we need to change. Many of our traditional ideas and practices would lead us automatically to discard this role and this kind of content, which is something we would be wise not to do. The next chapter looks at the unique challenges and benefits of web-based user-generated content, and its impact on our traditional notions of authority and control.

Notes

1 DeFaveri, Annette (2008) *The Community-Led Libraries Toolkit*. Vancouver: Working Together Project.
2 Ibid.
3 Ibid.
4 Universal McCann (2008) 'More than half of US adults text, blog, otherwise use social media', MarketingCharts.com; available at: *www.marketingcharts.com/interactive/more-than-half-of-us-adults-text-blog-otherwise-use-social-media-5502/* (accessed: 3 August 2008).
5 *RSA Journal* (2008) 'Online vote', *RSA Journal*, CLIV(5,533): 12.
6 Interested readers can request details of the survey results by e-mailing info@vpl.ca.
7 Perez, Sarah (2008) 'The next social networks will be powered by WordPress and Moveable Type', ReadWriteWeb, 14 August; available at: *www.readwriteweb.com/archives/the_next_social_networks_powered_by_wordpress_movable_type.php* (accessed: 3 August 2008).
8 See note 6 above.
9. See note 6 above.

3

A changing world

Web-based user-generated content is fundamentally different from much of the content that we typically work with in the information profession. As such, it brings with it some unique challenges and benefits. This chapter examines some of the more significant issues, and how they impact on us as librarians.

The wisdom of crowds versus the cult of the amateur

One of the most hotly debated issues surrounding Web 2.0 is whether the mass of information available on the internet, and the ease with which anyone can become an author and share their personal views with the world, is dumbing us down or making us smarter. This is an important issue for libraries: if there's no value in user-generated content, why would we invite it on to our websites?

This topic is significant enough that a number of books have already been published on it. Some of the seminal titles that support the value of user-generated content are *The Wisdom of Crowds* by James Surowiecki, *Everything Is Miscellaneous* by David Weinberger and *Ambient Findability* by Peter Morville. These titles lay out the evidence, as eloquently and convincingly as Steven Berlin Johnson did for video gaming, movies and mass media in *Everything Bad Is Good for You*,[1] that modern culture is not, in fact, making us stupid: it's making us smarter.

Surowiecki examines the quite astonishing evidence that when large numbers of people collaborate on a problem, they are invariably smarter than a few people, regardless of their personal brilliance, working independently. The group almost always come out with the right answer, no matter how extreme the odds against it might appear. Part of the reason for this is that when information is dispersed via a medium such as the internet, people are no longer reliant on their own personal knowledge. Instead, they have access to the collective wisdom and reaction of all of those people whose input has been collected and disseminated via the internet, enormously increasing the quantity of information and range of experiences that they have to draw upon. The crowd make smarter decisions than the individual, and the internet has increased the size of the crowd enormously.[2]

In *Everything Is Miscellaneous*, Weinberger examines information as a social asset and finds that, far from the volume of information overwhelming us and causing us to become lost in the digital jungle, the chances of us finding what we need increase when we have access to more information. This is true even when the information is not arranged according to any of our formal classification systems. He argues that these traditional classification systems used to organize information – and more than information, knowledge – have always been constrained by physical limitations, whether the layout of an office-supply store or the pages in an encyclopedia. Now, for the first time, the digital world allows us to organize knowledge with no physical restraints at all, freeing it from the limitations of fixed order and classification. Every piece of information can exist in multiple places, and be classified in every category to which it could conceivably belong. The result is that information has become an amorphous jumble, one into which we reach with the hooks of the digital age – keywords, Google searches, tags – and fish out what we need, rather than following a linear path to what we hope will be the right conclusion.[3]

Morville investigates how the modern internet, with its GPS applications, folksonomies and powerful search engines, has rendered every object and person in the world more findable. He argues that the internet is a rich source of new genres, disseminated information and increased collaboration. The result is that our cultural heritage has become more findable and we have become smarter and more informed, not just about searching the web but about how to interpret and analyze the results of those searches. Moreover, authority as we traditionally understand it is shifting from the institution to the individual. He also concludes, significantly, that this increased findability is fundamentally changing who we are: 'What we find changes who we become.'[4]

In the opposite corner is Andrew Keen with *The Cult of the Amateur*, an equally well-written polemic arguing against what he describes as a kind of overwhelmingly narcissistic internet culture, the unending noise of millions of blogging monkeys typing away at their laptops and never producing anything remotely like the works of Shakespeare. This culture, he argues, is leading to a blurring of the lines between fact and fiction, a casual disregard for copyright and intellectual property, and the devastation of traditional industries such as the music business and the news media.

> These millions and millions of exuberant monkeys – many with no more talent in the creative arts than our

> primate cousins – are creating an endless digital forest of mediocrity. For today's amateur monkeys can use their networked computers to publish everything from uninformed political commentary, to unseemly home videos, to embarrassingly amateurish music, to unreadable poems, reviews, essays and novels.[5]

Keen sees blogs at the heart of this downgrading of popular culture, pointing out that they are now so ubiquitous and so overwhelming in their sheer volume that they have eroded our ability to distinguish fact from fiction and permanently damaged 'the quality and reliability of the information we receive, thereby distorting, if not outrightly corrupting, our national civic conversation'.[6] The casualties of this tide of mediocrity are creative individuals and legitimate businesses: the musicians whose songs are being traded for free on file-sharing networks, the publishers whose encyclopedias are no longer selling because everyone with a computer has access to Wikipedia, the newspapers whose advertisers now post for free on Craigslist. In short, the people whose legitimate livelihoods and creative output are being either hijacked or drowned out by the sheer volume of these collected conversations.

(All four of these books are fascinating and extremely well written, and well worth reading in full by anyone interested in the evolution of information in the modern digital era.)

Keen puts his finger on what for us, as librarians, is one of our darkest fears about user-generated content. Is there really value in the conversation of the community? What if the user dialogue that we're inviting on to our websites is nothing more than meaningless noise, poor-quality, misspelled rantings that offer no value whatsoever? What if our sites become just one more platform for users to push their personal agendas or emotional outbursts? What if this destroys the credibility that we have built as providers of trusted information, of carefully built collections of hand-selected and individually annotated web links that provide a quality-rather-than-quantity approach which Google can't rival, of study guides that provide definitive information on a subject whether you're searching a stack of books, subscription databases or the entire internet? What if, by inviting user-generated content on to our sites, we're encouraging the cult of the amateur, sabotaging our own role as custodians of legitimate information and knowledge, and making a terrible, terrible mistake?

This has been a popular argument among naysayers since libraries first began to examine the possibility of utilizing Web 2.0 tools and inviting user-generated content into the library. And the contrast between Keen's views and those of Weinberger, Surowiecki and Morville highlights an interesting dichotomy about the internet itself: there's a multitude of evidence to support both points of view. You only have to browse a few popular social networking sites to find the cult of the amateur running rampant. Most blogs on MySpace are literally almost unreadable unless you're used to conversing in text speak; the odd intelligent response on Yahoo! Answers is usually buried among a plethora of syntactically nightmarish attempts at answers that are frequently inaccurate, plain wrong or completely unrelated to the question (and many of the questions are not much better); and the average collection of YouTube video comments (Figure 3.1) is so clueless and predictable that even webcomic Randall Munroe felt obliged to comment (Figure 3.2).

There's no question that there is an awful lot of dross out there on the internet, and picking your way through it to find the quality can be an uphill battle. Yahoo! Answers is perhaps one of the best examples of this (Figures 3.3

Figure 3.1 Sample comments from YouTube video 'Dirt Bike Hill Climb'

Source: www.youtube.com/watch?v=ht3DMDx1spo

and 3.4). It purports to deliver a community of experts, poised to answer any question on any topic. Yet it's not for nothing that *Slate* reviewer Jacob Leibenluft described it as 'a librarian's worst nightmare'.[7] Yahoo! Answers focuses very much on quantity over quality, leaving the genuinely good answers adrift in a sea of hopeless inaccuracies,

Figure 3.2 xkcd on YouTube comments

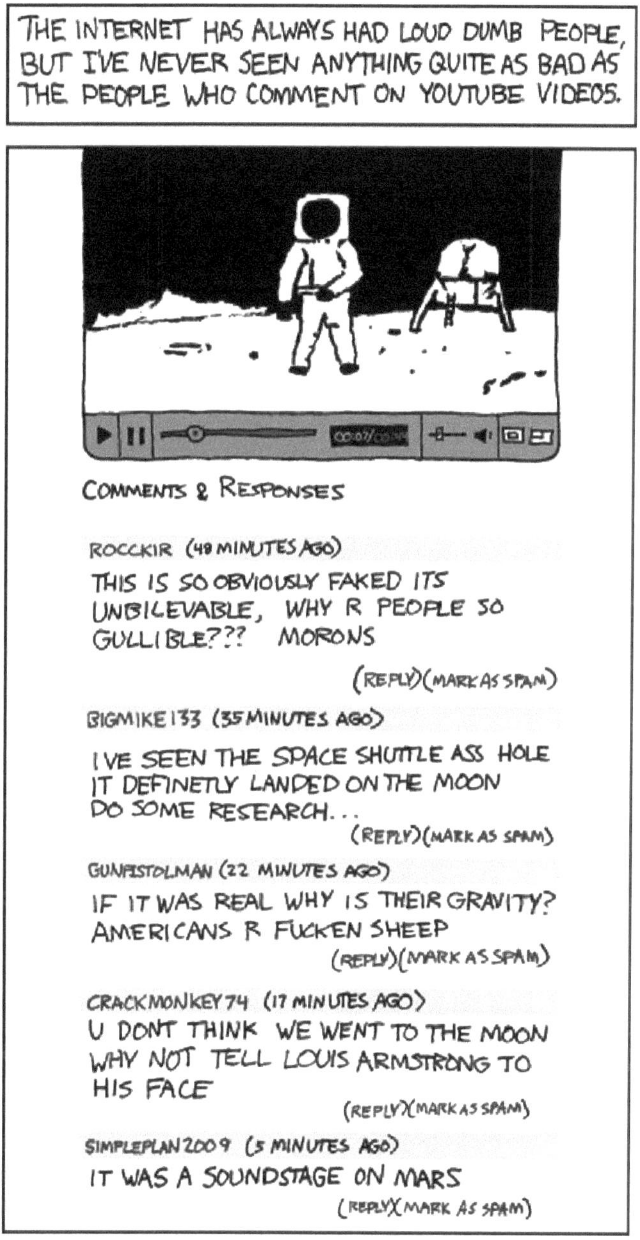

Source: http://xkcd.com/202/, courtesy of Randall Munroe

Figure 3.3 Yahoo! Answers: a concerned resident of Georgia, USA, seeks advice after reading media reports of the Russian invasion of Georgia, August 2008

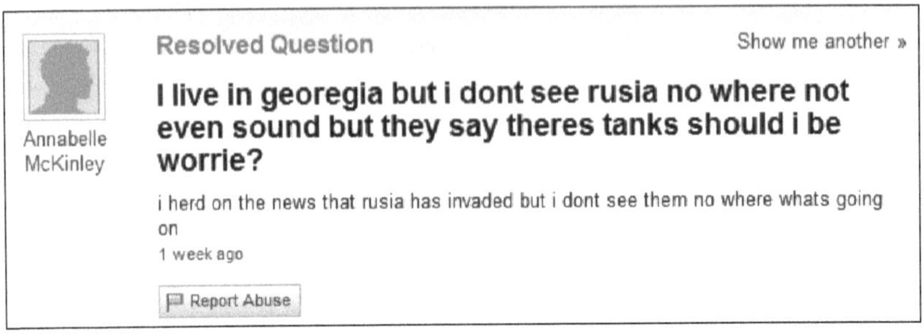

unsupported opinion and even – as in the case in Figures 3.5 and 3.6 – unprovoked vitriol. Any response, even one that's either plain wrong or completely unrelated to the topic, is rewarded with two points for the poster, encouraging users with nothing to say and no knowledge on the subject to post answers simply to reap the rewards. This practice is so commonplace that Yahoo! Answers users refer to it as 'point farming'.

Figure 3.4 Yahoo! Answers: at least he had enough sense to ask whether anyone else thought this was a good idea

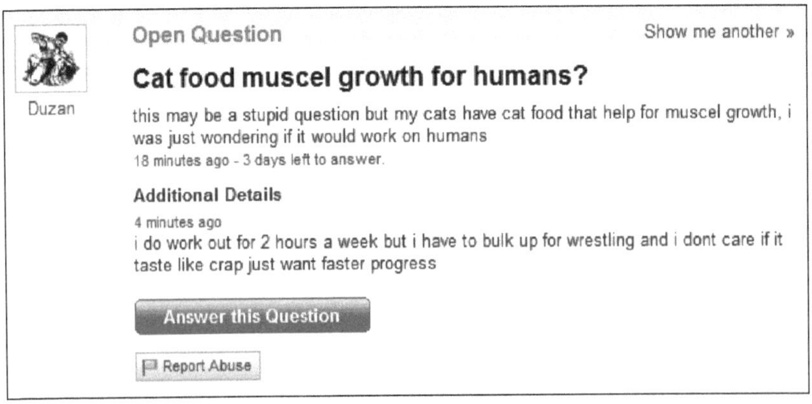

Figure 3.5 Yahoo! Answers: a sensitive question, showing the best answer (as chosen by the asker)

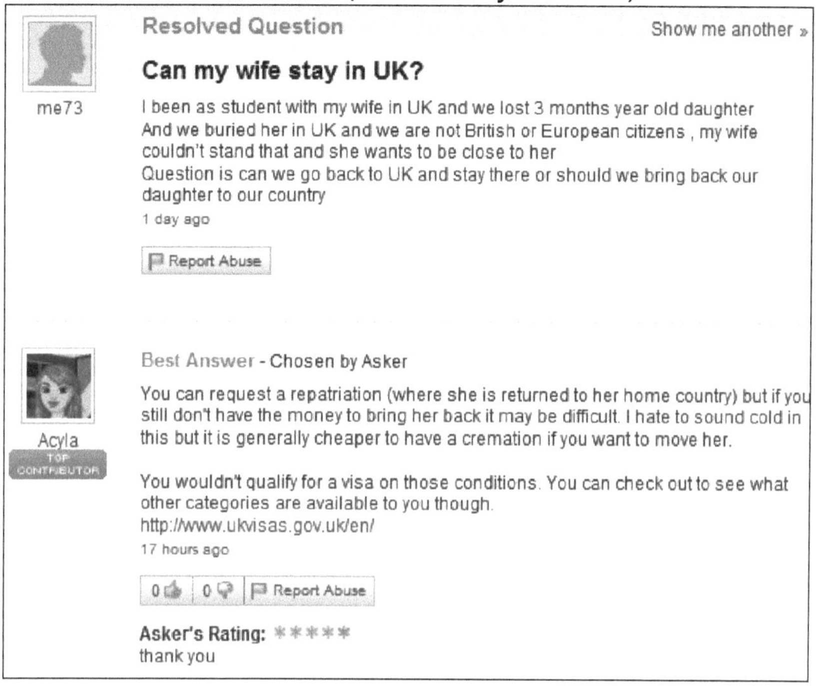

That's not to say that there aren't good answers hidden among the dross on Yahoo! Answers. In fact, a growing number of librarians, led by Bill Pardue from the Arlington Heights Memorial Library, have been participating in a monthly event called Slam the Boards since September 2007. On the tenth day of every month, interested librarians answer as many questions as possible on Yahoo! Answers, WikiAnswers, Askville and other 'answer board' sites. The idea is for the librarians to provide a high-quality, professional answer; and then market the added value that having a librarian answer the question has brought by promoting their own library or virtual reference service. Pardue exhorts participating librarians to 'surprise and delight them with our quality',[8] and this is exactly what

Figure 3.6 And a selection of the other answers

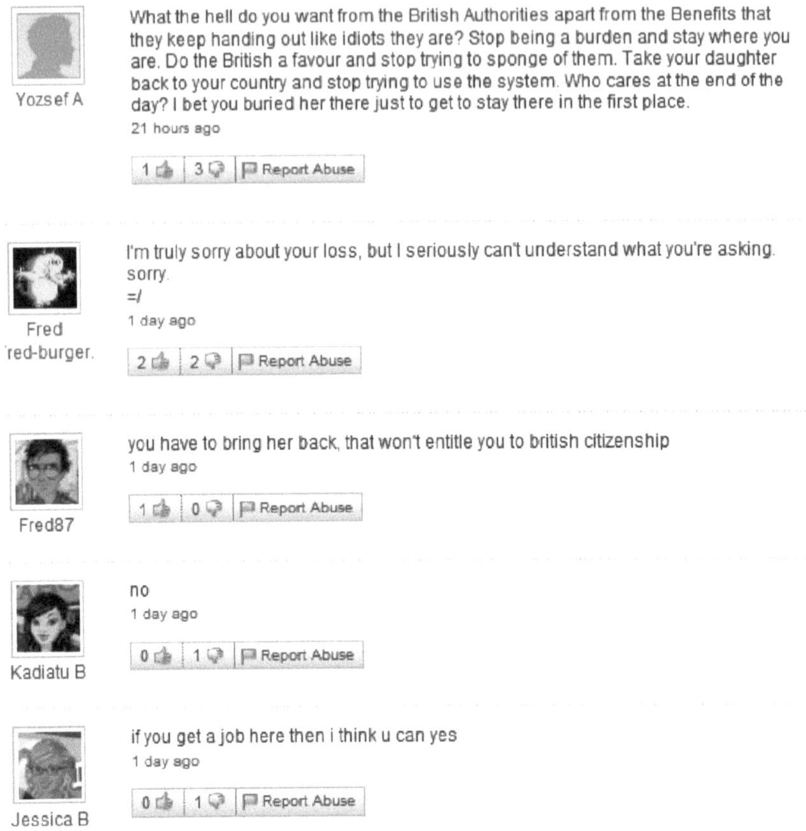

Slam the Boards has achieved, racking up numerous 'best answer' ratings and injecting some much-needed quality into the answer board services. But just like the quality answers that are coming from within the community, the danger is that the volume of noise surrounding these answers is such that most of them end up being drowned out.

It's also interesting, as someone who has personally been an active participant in many answer boards since the first Q&A services emerged online, to see just how the quality of these services has degenerated over time. Early answer boards – most notably WHnetworks' WHquestion.com and Clay Johnson's KnowPost.com – were notable for the high quality of the answers, and were commonly referred to as 'human encyclopedias'. While questions inevitably included a number that looked for opinion rather than answers, the responses were generally considered, well thought out and illuminating. What happened between 2001, when these sites shut down, and now? If we look at these sites as a microcosm of the wider web, has the growing volume of internet traffic – and more specifically, the migration to a truly read/write platform – really led to the dumbing down of internet content?

Numbers have certainly played a part. WHquestion in its heyday had 60,000 users; Yahoo! Answers has 60 million. The sheer volume of dialogue – questions, answers and overall words typed – is exponentially higher on Yahoo! Answers than it was on WHquestion (or any other answer board site, for that matter). With such a high volume of content being produced, it's inevitable that the signal-to-noise ratio will become significantly distorted. There are a lot of right answers in there, but they're being drowned out in the noise around them.

The reward scheme at Yahoo! Answers has also had a negative impact on content quality. Yahoo! Answers rewards users for participation, rather than for the quality of the answers they provide. At WHquestion rewards were dependent on the asker judging your answer as worthwhile, and answers that were marked irrelevant or incorrect actually cost users points. WHquestion also offered users material rewards (a set of coasters, a t-shirt and a personal user icon) once their points reached certain set levels, a model that would almost certainly be unsustainable on a site the size of Yahoo! Answers but which did provide users with an incentive to avoid poor ratings and the attendant point docking. While it makes sense to reward participation if you want to build content and encourage interaction, if you want to market yourself as a community of experts then there also needs to be an incentive for quality. (The ten points that Yahoo! offers for a 'best answer' rating doesn't seem sufficient to provide this, since the rating itself is entirely subjective and ten points can just as easily be racked up by posting five two-word responses.)

Part of the issue, too, is identified by Leibenluft: 'for millions of people on the Web, it's less important to get a good answer than to get someone to listen to your question in the first place'.[9] Yahoo! Answers is as much about the social interaction as it is about right and wrong answers. WHquestion and other answer boards of its era had communities, but the focus of the community was always on finding the most accurate or most complete answer to the latest question. While questions looking for other users' opinions were still posted regularly, the ratio of these opinion-based questions to fact-based questions (or what we would perceive as reference questions) was far lower than is currently the case on Yahoo! Answers. Quite simply, the focus has shifted: before it was on the question, and now it's on the community.

While at first this might appear to support Andrew Keen's concerns about the cult of the amateur taking over, in fact it's more of an object lesson for anyone starting an online community, or looking to engage a particular audience in dialogue. Make sure your community is focused, and try to stay true to that focus as the community evolves. Set your goals early – preferably before your community is even launched – and don't lose sight of them as you move forward. If necessary, develop policies to discourage off-topic posting. If you're offering rewards, make sure they encourage quality as well as quantity.

It's also worth keeping in mind that no matter how successful, a library-based community is very unlikely to accumulate 60 million active users. The smaller, more closely knit a community is, the easier it is to keep it focused. In fact, small-scale internet communities tend to develop a very strong sense of community ownership, and become effectively self-moderating. A community based around a library service – for example, a virtual book club – will attract people from within the relatively small demographic of that library's user base, and those people will likely have a strong shared interest in books, reading and other aspects of the library. Keeping this kind of small-scale community on topic and focused is an entirely different venture compared to the challenge of imposing any kind of regulation on 60 million users on a general answer board.

Moreover, an increasing volume of users doesn't necessarily mean that content will inevitably degenerate. Leibenluft compares the quality of Yahoo! Answers to Wikipedia,[10] which has also expanded enormously in recent years – it now boasts over 20 million articles and approximately 75,000 regular editors, plus many more sporadic contributors. At Wikipedia the community's focus is on ensuring that articles are accurate, unbiased and written from the all-important neutral point of view. Yahoo! Answers is all about volume; rather than correcting misinformation or building on incomplete answers, the focus is on providing a unique answer of your own. You can also use this answer to address errors in previous answers if you wish, but flagging their inaccuracies won't see them removed from the page – and won't necessarily stop the asker, who doesn't know any better, from choosing one of those incorrect answers as the 'best answer'.

Wikipedia, on the other hand, is concerned about keeping its articles accurate and unbiased rather than making them as lengthy as possible. The growing numbers of editors, rather than muddying the water with clouds of misinformation or opinion masquerading as fact, simply ensure that there are more eyes available to check out the latest contributions and, if needed, correct or remove problem information. The model is not infallible, with certain hot-button articles periodically falling victim to deliberate sabotage or editing wars, but Wikipedia is a very good example of how a different focus can result in a very different quality level. As Leibenluft points out, it says a great deal that Wikipedia is now considered worthy of direct comparison to the *Encyclopaedia Britannica*.[11]

To take a step back from this examination of particular sites and the quality of their content – because, after all, every website is different and no library community is going to reflect exactly the way content has evolved on a separate site with a unique user base and business model – it's worth returning to the broad view and looking at the vast increase in the overall amount of information that is now accessible to the general internet user. It is, to say the least, a morass: more webpages than we could ever hope to count, with such an endless cacophony of different points of view vying for attention that it's easy to believe that yes, this is nothing more than an overwhelming jumble of opinions from which it grows increasingly harder to draw out the facts.

The funny thing is that the opposite is actually true. The internet has been evolving in this direction for some time now, and as information seekers we're evolving along with it. We've learned that finding the answer is no longer necessarily about following a linear path from a to b, but about using keywords and search strings as the 'hooks' described by David Weinberger and casting them into the sea of information to bring back the content we need. As the read/write model has given more and more of us voices on the net, we've learned that it really is that easy to be an author: it's something any one of us with a computer and a connection to the internet can do. This makes us naturally more cautious of the content we find, and more inclined to look for some kind of credentials or verification – some kind of authority – that tells us we've found fact rather than fiction; the truth rather than just another unsubstantiated opinion. And in this context, I don't use 'we' to refer to information professionals, who through their very training have always exercised this kind of caution. I use it to refer to the general population of internet users, who are learning to appreciate the value in these information literacy principles and techniques.

It's particularly hard for the generation who didn't grow up with the internet to appreciate fully how substantially the overall attitude towards, and appreciation of, information has changed for the generation that's coming after us. We're too focused on the contrast between then and now, and too worried about the pitfalls that we see looming in the new world order. That's not actually quite how the current generation, the ones who grew up in the modern information environment – the Google world – see it. In their immensely readable and very educational article, 'Born with the chip', Stephen Abram and Judy Luther examine the key behavioral aspects of this generation, and their findings make for interesting reading.[12] The current generation are indifferent to form, expert multitaskers and able to adapt rapidly to new tools and technologies. They are experiential, nomadic and collaborative. When they're curious about a topic, they browse through the mass of information on the internet to find opinions and viewpoints on that topic from a huge range of people all around the world. They absorb and process these views and develop their own stand on the topic: they are principled.

Moreover, they're not drowning in the sea of information out there on the net: this volume of information is simply what they've always known. This environment and the tools required to negotiate it successfully are familiar. They know perfectly well that Dave the Janitor's blog is unlikely to give them the same kind of quality information as that of Dave the Harvard Professor. And they're smart enough to double-check Dave's credentials and make sure that he really does work for Harvard. They're not information illiterates who can't sort the wheat from the chaff: in fact, they're the most technically expert and information-literate generation that's ever existed.

Of course, there's always a down side. One other trait that Abram and Luther identified is that this generation are also very quick to move on when they don't find the answer they're looking for.[13] This is in part a reflection on the ubiquitous presence of Google, which has misled users into thinking that the answer is always a keyword away. It's also a natural response from a generation who are well aware that if they don't find the information in the first place they look, it's almost certainly going to exist in a multitude of other places. They can also be emo, aggravating, quick to dismiss other points of view and quick to anger. But is that really the exclusive preserve of teenagers on the internet? Are they behaving in any way that's different to the way they behave offline?

It's true that the modern net is a slew of fact, fiction, misinformation and opinion. But what's also true is that when we surf the net, whether it's for research or pleasure, we almost never look at the bigger picture. We have this incredible array of tools, ranging from Google to RSS to FriendFeed, to hook out or filter out the content that we're interested in. Like the impressive semantic filtering capabilities of Twine, we have the ability to bypass the dross entirely. We cast our hooks deeper to pull back the information we need, the relevant, interesting information that is just as significant a part of the net as the millions of blog posts made by Andrew Keen's typing monkeys.

And realistically, would we want to be without those blog posts? It's true that vast numbers of them are poorly written and contain no information of interest to anyone outside of the poster's immediate family and friends (and possibly not even to them), but there are innumerable blogs out there that contain valuable, useful information, whether they're sharing a breaking news story or analyzing the latest product to emerge from a San Francisco start-up. I learn an incredible amount every day from blogs posted by experts in their fields, or just people with keen eyes and bright minds who share some of my own interests. Just because a blog post is someone's opinion doesn't make it worthless or without value.

The question remains, though: all this conjecture is all very well and good, but what does this user-generated content – these blog posts, these discussions – bring to our websites? What's the purpose in the library becoming a facilitator and host for these kinds of dialogues?

They bring all the value-adds discussed in the previous chapter: they turn our websites into genuine community spaces, two-way dialogues where we learn more about our users as they learn more about the services we can offer them. They make us relevant and interesting to our users, and help keep us that way. They make us truly collaborative and open, and extend our reach far beyond our traditional buildings and web services. They enable us to embrace the intelligence of the masses, because it's out there on the net as well. Along with the monkeys posting incoherent responses to YouTube videos, the best minds of this generation and the next are blogging away, sharing information, and they have important things to tell us. They have important information to share.

There's another thing that we can do by opening ourselves up to user-generated content. We become a venue for online conversation. Lankes et al., in a recent article on libraries as participatory networks, explained the importance of this very effectively:

> Knowledge is created through conversation. Libraries are in the knowledge business. Therefore, libraries are in the conversation business. Some of those conversations span millennia, while others only span a few seconds. Some of these conversations happen in real time. In some conversations, there is a broadcast of ideas from one author to multiple audiences. Some conversations are sparked by a book, a video, or a web page. Some of these conversations are as trivial as directing someone to the bathroom. Other conversations center on the foundations of ourselves and our humanity.[14]

This is something we often neglect to consider: that conversation – dialogue – is the foundation of knowledge. Conversation is one of the key mechanisms by which we share ideas, and through which those ideas evolve. Conversation is part of our cultural memory and our community heritage. Libraries are, ultimately, in the conversation business. Opening our websites to conversation is not only a natural step, but it allows us to preserve that conversation for the future. And while it's true that we may end up reading and managing low-quality content, we'll inevitably find that we are also reading posts that are thought-provoking, interesting and ultimately propel us in new directions that we might not otherwise have explored. The read/write internet does pull in the worst of the content that people create, but that shouldn't cause us to ignore the fact that it also pulls in the best.

Low-fidelity authority

Web 2.0, or the participatory web, is forcing information professionals to rethink many core aspects of our profession. It's had profound changes on the kind of information that we deal with on a day-to-day basis, on the way we search that information and on the way our users view both themselves and the information environment. We're seeing some cataclysmic changes in classification schemata with the rise of the folksonomy, where users build a bottom-up system of natural language tags to classify content rather than the traditional top-down hierarchies of the library world. Our views on intellectual property and copyright are shifting. We're also having to rethink our traditional views of authority.

Traditional authority, like traditional classification schemes, operates within a very clear set of rules and boundaries. They are the boundaries we try to teach our users in information literacy sessions, or when we're explaining the value of a library-purchased subscription database over a Google search, of a peer-reviewed journal over a blog. Authority means reliability; authority means credibility (Figure 3.7). Authority is definitive. Authority adds value.

The danger with this traditional view of authority is that we end up discarding, or ignoring, the value in the user-created content generated by these new participatory networks. We can see this in Andrew Keen's book, where he completely dismisses the credibility of Wikipedia as a source

Figure 3.7 Sites like Suite101.com, where this article was originally posted, add credibility to user-generated content by including traditional reference lists… sometimes to the surprise of their audience

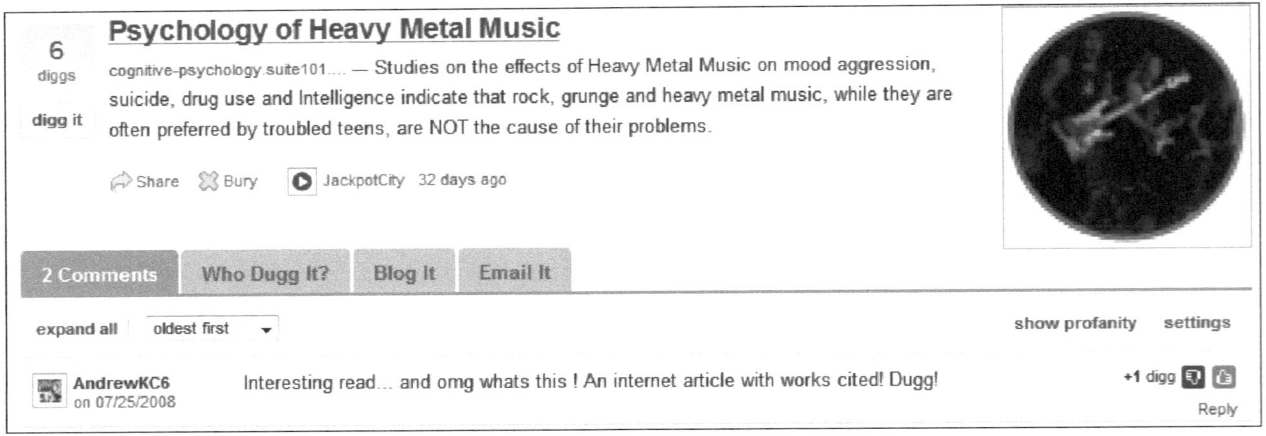

Source: http://digg.com/music/Psychology_of_Heavy_Metal_Music

because of the lack of available credentials (and ability to check those credentials) of its army of editors. Yet we're talking about a resource that, as mentioned previously, has been held up for detailed comparison with the *Encyclopaedia Britannica*, and was found to be only marginally less accurate than the articles produced by *Britannica*'s 4,000 paid contributors and 300 editors and fact-checkers.

Should we dismiss Wikipedia entirely simply because we don't know, or can't verify, the credentials and expertise of its contributors? Is Andrew Keen right when he argues that Wikipedia is 'the blind leading the blind... perpetuating the cycle of misinformation and ignorance'?[15] Or should we be listening to Jimmy Wales, co-founder of Wikipedia, when he says 'The key thing is getting it right. I don't care if they're a high school kid or a Harvard Professor.'[16]

The answer, as it so often is, is that the truth lies somewhere in the middle. Of course traditional authority brings value: a unique value that lends immediate credibility to an authoritative source or reference. But there is also value – a different kind of value – in 'getting it right' regardless of credentials. We dismiss that value at our peril; it means dismissing a vast amount of potentially useful (even crucial, in some instances) information. There is also value in carefully crafted, thoughtful and thought-provoking opinion. It is these opinions that spur conversation, reflection, dialogue; it is these opinions that we discuss and challenge, and by which we ultimately increase the breadth of our own knowledge. They help us define where we stand on issues; they inform our world view.

It's true that getting it right, or analyzing something in an interesting manner, does not give us the kind of immediate reassurance that a peer-reviewed journal or carefully assembled list of relevant, easily checked references does.

Instead, what we need to do is accept that in the age of distributed authorship and user-generated content, there is more than one kind of authority. There is the authority that comes from having the appropriate credentials, and then there is the authority that comes from being what is perhaps best described as a 'community expert' – or, in other words, the person who gets it right.

These people might not have a degree or official accreditation; there are no letters after their names. What they will have is one or more of the following. They have excellent research skills, honed by hours of browsing the net or the shelves of their local library. They're adept and experienced enough to be well aware of where the fallacies are online, and what content they should trust and what they should take with a grain of salt. Or maybe they have a unique breadth and depth of experience in a personal pastime or a passion. Or perhaps they have a natural flair for analysis, for seeing to the heart of an issue. They are able to process and disseminate information quickly and accurately. They share their skills and knowledge on sites like Wikipedia, Suite101 or maybe their own personal blogs. They cite their sources so that we can judge for ourselves the degree of their expertise. They produce content that's interesting, truthful and right. Their readers value their work and learn from it.

This kind of community expertise is not the same thing as traditional authority. But it has immense value and should not be summarily dismissed. This community expertise is *low-fidelity authority*. It's not as refined and perfect as traditional authority. It's less predictable, rougher around the edges. It doesn't come with a guarantee of quality; we double-check it, and look at the sources that informed the Wikipedia article or the reference list on the Suite101 post. It's not quite as polished. But it's more easily accessible and more widely distributed. It's about natural language rather than academic jargon; about individual experience rather than formal research. It's democracy over élitism; it's the unsigned band distributing their own material rather than the next big thing owned part and parcel by the record company. It's about content that facilitates swift engagement and ongoing interest. It's authority for the masses.

Embracing this kind of value and this redefined notion of authority helps us reach that pot of gold at the end of the rainbow: it helps us remain relevant and accessible to our users. It helps us stay in touch with what they think and what they want from their library. If we become too wedded to the idea that the internet is all about dumbing down, we run the risk of losing all that value, all the community expertise and the opportunities to share, to discuss and to challenge ourselves. When we focus too much on the noise, we lose track of the meaningful signal within it.

Andrew Keen states that we create 'structures of authority... so that we know we can trust what we read'.[17] This is true. But authority in the age of distributed authorship is a two-tier system, and to some extent it's up to us to define that second tier, the low-fidelity authority. As information professionals we can help educate people on the principles of information literacy that help them understand what information they shouldn't trust online. We can help them see the different kinds of value that can be drawn from the different kinds of information they discover. We can teach them to use the tools that sift this information, that sort it, that cast the hooks that draw in the pieces they need. Our role has undergone a seismic shift from the gatekeepers of old to facilitators and teachers: guides to the new information environment.

Unverified information can be genuinely very misleading, especially where the author makes an effort to dress it up as fact, as in the Lasik@Home example shown in Figure 3.8. But in terms of teachable moments, it doesn't come much better than this site. Teaching a class on information literacy, or on finding information online? Ask your patrons to analyze this website. Point out the obvious flaws: the lack of standard contact information like a phone number or mailing address; the inability actually to order the product using the 'Order Now' tab. Carry out a very simple Google search – the name of the site is sufficient, without quotes – and point out that the third item to show up is a Snopes story discrediting the site as a hoax (www.snopes.com/inboxer/hoaxes/lasikathome.asp). Introduce Snopes and explain its value as a source for checking the veracity of urban legends, rumors, e-mail forwards and other pieces of misinformation that abound on the internet. Use opportunities like Lasik@Home and anonymous, unverified blogs to teach people to have a critical eye, to be reasonably confident in making a swift assessment of a source's reliability and to identify resources where their trust is not misplaced.

Andrew Keen states that user-generated content has led to a situation where 'with more and more of the information online unedited, unverified and unsubstantiated, we will have no choice but to read everything with a sceptical eye'.[18] In his view, this is a terrible thing. It sucks up our time and causes confusion and bewilderment as we struggle to make sense of information we can't possibly trust.

This is possible, and no doubt we've all been fooled by a credible-looking source at one time or another, or cursed the time we've wasted on a search where we simply haven't been able to pull out the fact from the fiction. But looking at everything with a skeptical eye isn't necessarily a bad thing. The general populace is smart enough and experienced enough at web searching to know perfectly well that a

Figure 3.8 Misinformation masquerading as fact

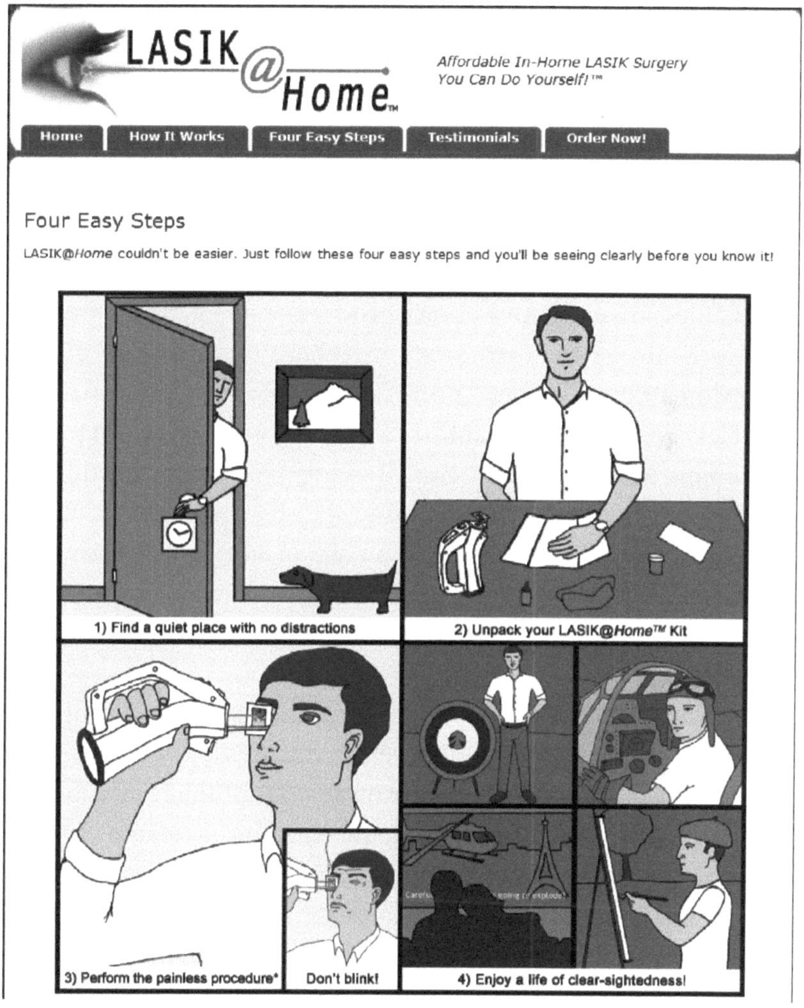

Source: www.lasikathome.com/foureasysteps.htm

completely unsubstantiated blog post by an anonymous author isn't something that we can trust, cite in a research article or base our political vote on. What we can do is look at that blog post with our skeptical eye, and assess it. Is the author obviously placing a particular spin on the story? What are they trying to make us believe? Why? What can we find that supports their point of view? What can we find that contradicts it?

We must also stop being so afraid of making mistakes. Was it a mistake to encourage the read/write web, to flood the internet with user-generated content? It's certainly contributed a lot of misinformation to the general pool: opinion masquerading as fact, advertising masquerading as fact and even advertising masquerading as opinion, in cases like the number of viral YouTube videos that were actually planted by companies with products to sell. Sure, life was more straightforward when information was more clearly delineated. Fiction, non-fiction, movies, newspapers, television: things fell into neat little boxes, rather than this jumble we face today. But drawing sense from the jumble has taught us a lot, and continues to teach us every time we go searching. We learn as much, if not more, from our mistakes as we do from our successes. If we're fooled by a fraudulent article, or taken in by a hoax, we're much less likely to make that same mistake again.

One of the core Web 2.0 philosophies is the perpetual beta state, or continuous improvement process. This is used to describe a product that never moves out of the testing phase: its creators pilot by making the product available to end users, solicit constant feedback and use that feedback to inform changes to the product that make it better: more efficient, more user-friendly, more useful. In terms of our own navigation of the internet, we're now in a process of perpetual beta. We search, we learn, we refine our search techniques. We increase our understanding of how information is presented on the web, and what we can trust and what we can't. We learn from our successes, and we learn from our mistakes. We continue to improve.

A culture of sharing

Libraries take their role as custodians of their patrons' personal information very seriously. Our traditional stance has been as fierce guardians of user privacy, very aware of our legal and ethical obligations to people who trust us not just with their personal information – names, addresses, dates of birth – but with the record of the books they have borrowed and the websites that they browse when they use the library's internet terminals.

In the modern world our ethical and legal obligations to protect user privacy have been placed in the spotlight as never before. We've all seen news stories about plucky librarians resisting FBI demands for computer records under Patriot Act legislation (Figures 3.9 and 3.10).

There's an interesting dichotomy between this traditional role as the guardian of user privacy and our efforts to embrace the Web 2.0 model, where the focus is very much on sharing. Social networking is all about sharing your information – your photographs, your videos and your

Figure 3.9 Librarian challenges FBI

Library Challenges FBI Request

Patriot Act Prohibits Details of Lawsuit From Being Released

By Dan Eggen
Washington Post Staff Writer
Friday, August 26, 2005; Page A11

A member of the American Library Association has sued the Justice Department to challenge an FBI demand for records, but the USA Patriot Act prohibits the plaintiff from publicly disclosing its identity or other details of the dispute, according to court documents released yesterday.

Source: www.washingtonpost.com/wp-dyn/content/article/2005/08/25/AR2005082501696.html

Figure 3.10 Patriot Act invades privacy

Librarian Who Resisted FBI Says Patriot Act Invades Privacy

By Andrew Miga
Associated Press
Thursday, April 12, 2007; Page A12

A librarian who fended off an FBI demand for computer records on patrons said Wednesday that secret anti-terrorism investigations strip away personal freedoms.

Source: www.washingtonpost.com/wp-dyn/content/article/2007/04/11/AR2007041102041.html

opinions. It's about letting people know what you're doing right now this minute, and the minute after, and the minute after that. With the growing popularity of sites like Facebook and LinkedIn that focus on real-life connections, it's also become more acceptable to post your personal information – name, phone number, place of work – online. While safety advocates (and common sense) tell us that it's not smart to post information like this on the open net, we're willing to share it within these sites because they are to some extent walled gardens. But the walls are not that high and people can easily look over; unless you take the time to go into Facebook's or LinkedIn's privacy features and lock down the information that's publicly available, anyone browsing the net can still see your public profile.

A surprisingly large number of people don't take the time to screen this information, and also don't much care. In a world where more and more information is easily accessible online (Google my name, for example, and you immediately have access to the public listing of my job, phone number and work e-mail, not to mention every post I ever made to a number of library listservs), people are becoming less guarded about seeing odd pieces of personal information on the web, especially those that relate solely to our professional lives. We save our caution for the items that can cause real-world damage: bank details, credit card information, Social Security numbers.

People are particularly cavalier about sharing their personal tastes and opinions. Amazon has been an interesting example of this: it was one of the first truly mainstream sites to share user reviews, ratings, user-assembled lists of recommended titles and aggregated discovery information that helps readers find new books by recommending titles purchased by people who share their tastes. LibraryThing, Shelfari and Facebook's Visual Bookshelf all provide even more tools to support this trend, passing along recommendations and encouraging people to replicate their entire physical book collection online so that it can be shared by the community.

This, of course, is entirely different to having the FBI approach a public library and demand that it hands over patrons' reading records. It's one thing to choose voluntarily which books from your collection you want to share online; quite another to have everything you've ever borrowed from the library handed over to a government agency without your consent. However, the danger is that libraries have traditionally guarded their users' privacy so fiercely that it may end up restricting our ability to offer the kinds of services that people really want to use. We've heard from our patrons, and what they're interested in is seeing the catalogue become a true readers' advisory and discovery tool. We heard this at Vancouver Public Library when we surveyed our users to see what they wanted in a new library website.[19] Gail Richardson of Oakville Public Library heard it loud and clear when it made the decision to purchase BiblioCommons. 'People don't want a library that acts like just a glorified card catalog online. They want a catalog that's as good as Google and Amazon.'[20] It's what Hennepin County Library wanted to achieve when it created Bookspace, an online community for patrons to share and review books. The uptake that both Oakville and Hennepin are seeing in the social discovery tools they have built into – or layered over – the traditional catalogue is proof of a real appetite for this kind of information sharing among library patrons.

In 2007 the OCLC conducted a detailed study on 'Sharing, privacy and trust in our networked world'.[21] The results reveal a fascinating paradigm shift between the ways in which librarians and patrons view patron privacy.

Just 11 per cent of surveyed users felt their activity on a library's website was private or very private; this compared to the 63 per cent who felt that online banking is private or very private. Use of a library's web collection was also viewed as very private by 11 per cent of respondents; use of a library's print collection was seen as very private by just 9 per cent. Social discovery activities – searching and browsing – were generally not regarded as being private. Seventy-five per cent of respondents felt it was important for the library to keep personal information private, but this dropped to between 40 per cent and 50 per cent who thought it was important to keep private such activities as the items viewed on the library website, items borrowed from print collections and reference questions asked in person and online.

More interesting trends emerge when looking at the situations in which users are willing to share personal information. Around a quarter of users are prepared to share personal contact information if it helps them connect with people with similar interests, or if there's another trade-off in terms of receiving a more personalized service or free goods and services. Respondents were concerned that they retain control over how much information they share online, and the option to remain anonymous if desired.

So far, nothing completely unexpected: we live in a networked world, and people are becoming more used to a culture of sharing non-essential information. Users are aware of the difference between discovery information and the benefits it brings, and truly private information – for example, banking details – that carries huge risks if it's made public.

Where the study gets really interesting is when it compares the views of librarians to the views of the general public. Librarians are more concerned about internet privacy than their users, and consistently overestimate the level of concern over online privacy among their users. Almost half of the surveyed library directors – 48 per cent – felt that their patrons would view a record of books they had read to be very private information, whereas only 16 per cent of patrons felt this was the case. Likewise, 50 per cent of directors thought that their patrons would feel their borrowing record was very private, whereas only 19 per cent of the public actually felt this way.

Library directors are also extremely aware of their role as guardians of patron privacy, and the significance of this responsibility to their users – to the extent where they guard patrons' personal information more closely than some patrons feel is necessary. Fewer than 20 per cent of library directors would be prepared to share details of patrons' browsing and borrowing patterns, even to help them connect with other people with similar interests, although almost half of users felt this was not information that it is important to keep private. This reluctance would severely restrict these libraries from being able to offer opportunities for participatory involvement and social discovery via their web services.

An interesting corollary to this is that library directors are consistently less likely than their patrons to make use of social networking spaces on the web, other than for work purposes. While directors are as heavily – if not more – active on the web when it comes to searching, browsing and shopping, they are less likely to use social sites for building relationships with other people. The report concludes that 'these... differences may explain the hesitancy of many librarians to enter into social networking when compared to other Internet activities that they embraced and often pioneered. As a group, librarians are using social spaces measurably less than their communities.'[22]

The results of this report are fascinating, and highlight the need for us to engage directly with our patrons to find out what they want from library services, and the degree to which they're prepared to share information to achieve this. We can't make assumptions about what we think they want, especially in a rapidly evolving environment where views are changing all the time. It's an interesting line for us to try to walk, balancing our responsibility to protect our users' privacy against the possibility of offering new services that will encourage them to engage with the library. As the study found, it's crucial to ensure that if people are able to make personal information available in return for a trade-off – relationship building, social discovery – the system is opt in rather than opt out, and that users always retain control of what information is available and the right to remain anonymous if they choose.

Setting boundaries in a world without borders

One of the key differences between the internet and offline life is the lack of physical and geographical boundaries.

Unlike a physical collection, which is limited to the footprint of the library and the number of units of shelving that can be fitted into it, there are no constraints on a web collection. (A number of libraries let this unexpected and unfamiliar freedom go to their heads in the 1990s, and the result was some very bloated library websites.) Likewise, there are no geographic boundaries on the web. The foot traffic on library websites comes from all over the world.

This is an issue for participatory web services because we're inviting people to contribute actively to our sites without necessarily having any assurance that they are, in fact, our library patrons. This problem has also raised its head for virtual reference services, and many require some form of user validation to prove that users are in fact from the appropriate location. Ohio's KnowItNow and Maryland's AskItNow, for example, both require users to enter their zip code before submitting a question.

The trouble with requiring some kind of patron authentication is that, as noted earlier, it's a known barrier to access. Requiring a postal code or library card number to be entered penalizes users who have no fixed address or who don't have a library card. While this might encourage some people to get a card, others will simply turn around at the barrier, walk away and never return.

The question is, are we genuinely concerned about having non-patrons interact on our websites? Early indicators are mixed. Hennepin County Library allows anyone to register and begin creating book lists and posting reviews; Toronto allows open registration for its BookBuzz discussion board. Oakville, on the other hand, requires an initial registration that includes the user's library card number; an important security measure as its BiblioCommons installation includes a single login that gives users access to both social tools and

My Account information. (It also makes it easier for users by allowing them to create a user name for future logins.)

Moreover, we welcome users who are not our regular patrons into our physical library spaces. When visitors from out of town walk through the doors of our Central Library here in downtown Vancouver, they have free access to the millions of books in our collection. They are provided with guest logins so that they can access the internet free of charge from the library's computer terminals. They have full access to all of our subscription electronic resources as long as they are in the library. They are most welcome to attend any of our free programs and training courses. They may only be in the city for a few days or weeks, but they walk away with a positive impression of a welcoming, inclusive library. We may not provide them with access to quite the full range of services – for example, the borrowing privileges – but we welcome their presence and any contribution they wish to make, whether joining in a program or commenting on a service. We welcome their participation in the physical space, the library community, and it seems only logical to extend this welcome online into whatever communities we establish there.

Libraries overall have become more cooperative and consortial in recent years, with collaborations of different library services offering everything from open source catalogue development (Evergreen) to 24-hour virtual reference services (AskColorado). Consortial database purchasing, like the model used in British Columbia where a core suite of databases are purchased by the Public Library Services Branch and then made available through every library in the province, can provide substantial savings as well as giving smaller libraries a unique opportunity to increase the scope of their collections and offer products they would not otherwise be able to afford. Partnerships like

InterLINK enable open access to member libraries, facilitating ease of use for patrons across geographic boundaries (for example, by enabling borrowing and returning privileges across a wider area so that patrons who live in one municipality but work in another can use both library services seamlessly). Libraries understand the value of sharing.

Libraries are also not competitive. We all have our distinct demographic boundaries, and there's no benefit for us in attempting to poach other libraries' patrons. What we want is to create better experiences for our own patrons, reach more non-users within our catchment area and create a positive impression of library services for everyone. Keeping our virtual doors wide open, rather than trying to filter the guests, is by far the better way to do this. The evidence shows that the more use a social network receives, and the more content it offers, the more its users engage and participate. Witness, for example, the phenomenal rise of Facebook when it stopped being a closed shop limited to universities and colleges. To make social web experiences meaningful and interesting for our patrons, we need to build a crowd of participants and a collection of interesting, engaging content.

Imagine a sharing model so large scale that library users browsing the catalogue won't just see ratings and comments from their own library, but from anyone across the province who has rated that particular book. Where a patron won't just be able to view booklists created by people who use their local library service, but lists from library users across the country. Imagine the wealth of information and data that could be shared in a model this large, the conversations and accumulated knowledge that could result. A grand vision for the future? Yes, and one that BiblioCommons expects to make a reality sooner rather than later.

The internet is all about bringing down boundaries. It's about exploring opinions that range far beyond your own social circle of work, school, family, hobbies: it's about exposing yourself to ideas and points of view that you might never have encountered without it. The value-add for information – the tipping point where it becomes knowledge and even wisdom – so often comes through its exposure to others, its dissection and reassembly during a lively discussion, the pieces that other people bring to it when it becomes the topic of conversation.

What's more, while there's a legitimate (if somewhat narrow-minded) argument that by providing access to users from outside our catchment area, we're doing a disservice to taxpayers, the same does not necessarily apply to web services. If other users wear out or lose books, these are no longer available to the taxpayers who funded them; if they access subscription databases, they're making free use of a service towards which they did not contribute. However, if you open a discussion group and have 50 users from your city and four Australian college students sign up, it makes no material difference. You don't have to invest staff time in building a new discussion board just for the students; all you have are more comments, which will hopefully encourage more people to participate. The only significant change in effort is that the more users you have the more time you will need to invest in moderation, but the pay-off is in the creation of more content reflecting a wider range of points of view: a more dynamic and engaging community.

We're under no obligation to make our participatory web services open to all. But restricting access for users who don't hold a library card, or who don't live in the appropriate municipality or district, closes a window to the wider world. It's not that we need to set boundaries when this world has no borders: more that we need to embrace the potential that the space offers us.

Bridging the divide

One thing we need to be extremely cognizant of as we work to develop opportunities for interaction and participation on our websites is that we don't end up increasing the digital divide. For people who have neither access to computers nor the skills to participate in online communities, these services are irrelevant and inaccessible.

We have it within our power to remedy this. To discuss the steps we can take to help bridge the digital divide in full would be an entire book – if not two – on its own, so I'll just run through a few basics here.

First of all, we must go out into the community to find these users and convince them that the library is relevant and meaningful for them. We need to enter a dialogue with them and find out what services we can offer that might be helpful to them.

To use an example from my own experience, I spent time a couple of years ago volunteering at the Women's Center on Vancouver's poverty-stricken and addiction-decimated downtown Eastside, providing assistance in its small computer room. For many of the women attending the center, these brief periods of access to four working machines were their only chance to use a computer that week. At the start I wasn't sure what the volunteering might involve, but imagined I would spend time on the same sort of internet skills that we provide via public training sessions at VPL: setting up e-mail, adding attachments, searching Google.

Instead, I found that the most common question that arose was how to use online job sites effectively. Many of the women who used the center were recovering from periods of addiction, and their next goal was steady employment. And as one of them, Beth (not her real name), pointed out to me, 'I'm much more likely to get an interview by applying online. If I walk into a restaurant with a help wanted sign, they can *see* that I live on the street.' One of Beth's other difficulties was that she did not have regular enough access to the internet to be able to respond to e-mails promptly, and when I spoke with her she had just missed out on an opportunity as a result. Beth was not someone who had been offered many opportunities in her life, and it was clear how much of a blow this was.

I explained that she was very welcome to use the computers at the public library any time she needed. She was grateful, and surprised; she wasn't a library user, and hadn't realized that the service was freely available even though her lack of a fixed address meant that she couldn't get a library card. I saw Beth at the Central Library a couple of times over the next few months, and the last time I ran into her she was leaving by Greyhound for a job at a hotel in Jasper a few days later. She laughed as she said she'd never imagined herself living in Jasper, but that was the other thing about being able to apply for jobs online: she had access to a much larger number of positions than she would have during a traditional job hunt. Reconnecting Beth with the library after more than 30 years had played a part in helping her successfully land a job, thanks also to some considerable persistence on her part. I very much hope the job worked out for her, and she continues her successful recovery.

WiFi and home broadband are so widespread now that we can sometimes forget how important free library internet access is to users who have no computer access of their own.

By making computers available to our users, we can provide them with access not just to the library website, but the whole world of dialogue and knowledge on the web. More importantly, we can share our skills to help them appreciate just how much they have access to through these computers, and how life-changing it can be. It can be frustrating to be a librarian on the reference desk and receive yet another question about how to add an attachment to an e-mail rather than something that truly tests our research skills. But that e-mail and attachment might be the single biggest thing in the day of the person sending it, or the recipient. These small assistances that we can so easily provide often make an enormous difference, especially if we take enough time to show patrons how to complete the task for themselves next time, and the time after, and the time after that.

Library training sessions are another option for us to share our skills with our patrons, but it's worth remembering that not all patrons are comfortable coming to traditional classroom-style sessions. This is an opportunity for us to go out into the community and develop training delivery mechanisms that work for users who may not feel comfortable coming to the library for a formal training session. Working Together staff, for example, found that members of the Indian Metis Christian Fellowship were very reluctant to attend training sessions in a computer lab, but were enthused and happy to learn when laptops were made available at a regular coffee time.[23]

The new world

It's not easy trying to get used to a completely new world. Some of the adjustments we need to make are pretty fundamental. Low-fidelity authority, the value in community expertise, a generation born with the chip: these are some quite radical changes. It's important that we remain aware of the negative sides of the internet, and the potential pitfalls of welcoming user-generated content into our libraries; but it's even more important to ensure that these things don't blind us to the positive side. If we allow that to happen, we have a lot to lose.

Notes

1 Johnson, Steven Berlin (2005) *Everything Bad Is Good for You: How Today's Popular Culture Is Actually Making Us Smarter*. New York: Riverhead Books.
2 Surowiecki, James (2005) *The Wisdom of Crowds*. Toronto: Random House of Canada.
3 Weinberger, David (2007) *Everything Is Miscellaneous*. New York: Holt Paperbacks.
4 Morville, Peter (2005) *Ambient Findability*. Sebastopol: O'Reilly Media.
5 Keen, Andrew (2008) *The Cult of the Amateur*. New York: Doubleday.
6 Ibid.
7 Leibenluft, Jacob (2007) 'A librarian's worst nightmare: Yahoo! Answers, where 120 million users can be wrong', *Slate*, 7 December; available at: *www.slate.com/id/2179393/* (accessed: 3 August 2008).
8 Pardue, Bill (2007) 'Slam the boards', Answer Board Librarians, August; available at: *http://answerboards.wetpaint.com/page/Slam+the+Boards!?t=anon* (accessed: 3 August 2008).
9 Leibenluft, note 7 above.
10 Ibid.
11 Ibid.
12 Abram, Stephen and Luther, Judy (2004) 'Born with the chip: growing up in a Google world', *Library Journal*, 1 May; available at: *www.libraryjournal.com/article/CA411572.html* (accessed: 3 August 2008).

13 Ibid.
14 Lankes, R. David, Silverstein, Joanne, Nicholson, Scott and Marshall, Todd (2007) 'Participatory networks: the library as conversation', *Information Research*, 12(4); available at: *http://InformationR.net/ir/12-4/colis05.html* (accessed: 3 August 2008).
15 Keen, note 5 above.
16 Ibid.
17 Ibid.
18 Ibid.
19 Interested readers can request details of the survey results by e-mailing info@vpl.ca.
20 Richardson, Gail (2008) 'BiblioCommons emerges: "revolutionary" social discovery system for libraries', *Library Journal*, 19 July; available at: *www.libraryjournal.com/article/CA6579748.html* (accessed: 3 August 2008).
21 De Rosa, Cathy, Cantrell, Joanne, Havens, Andy, Hawk, Janet and Jenkins, Lillie (2007) *Sharing, Privacy and Trust in Our Networked World*. Dublin: OCLC.
22 Ibid.
23 DeFaveri, Annette (2008) *The Community-Led Libraries Toolkit*. Vancouver: Working Together Project.

4

Drinking from the firehose

So what exactly are libraries doing with Web 2.0 tools and technologies? Quite a lot: some of it basic and straightforward, some of it pushing into new and innovative territory. Some things are small scale, quick and easy; others are changing the face of such core applications as the library catalogue. This chapter examines some of the ways in which libraries are using Web 2.0 tools to deliver services in the online space.

Library of Congress and Flickr

The Library of Congress is using Flickr, the photo-sharing site, as a platform to use community expertise to enhance its metadata (www.flickr.com/photos/library_of_congress/). With the goal of investigating how social tagging and online communities might benefit both the library and users of its collections, it took 3,000 images for which no copyright restrictions exist, uploaded the pictures to the library's Flickr account and invited users to tag and comment on them (Figure 4.1). The results have been phenomenal: in one month alone the page was viewed 5.4 million times; more than 10,000 unique tags were added to pictures; and the Library of Congress acquired more than 11,000 Flickr contacts on its network.

The library placed one single tag, 'Library of Congress', on each photograph. While it reserves the right to remove

Figure 4.1 The LoC photostream on Flickr

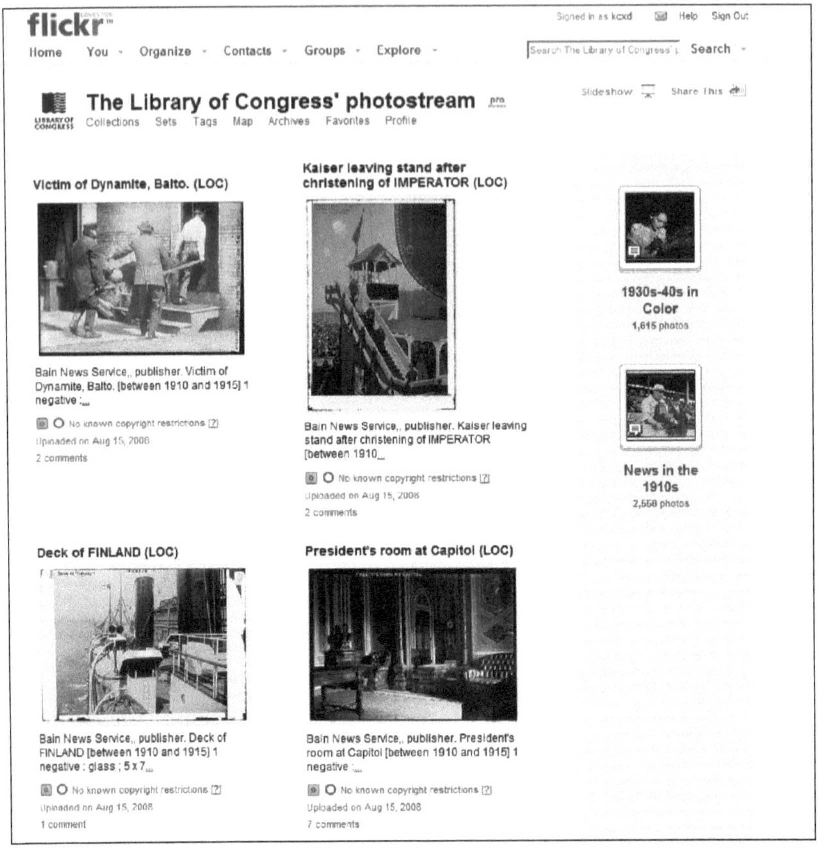

incorrect or inappropriate content, it has largely left the addition, control and management of tags down to the community (Figure 4.2).

Opening up its collection to the community on Flickr turned out to be not only a fantastic promotional mechanism for the library, which was able to reach many users who did not visit the official Library of Congress website and had thus had no opportunity to view its collections, but also a way of capturing key information that was missing from the original photograph records. With millions of viewers looking at the pictures, the potential to

Figure 4.2 LoC Flickr tag cloud

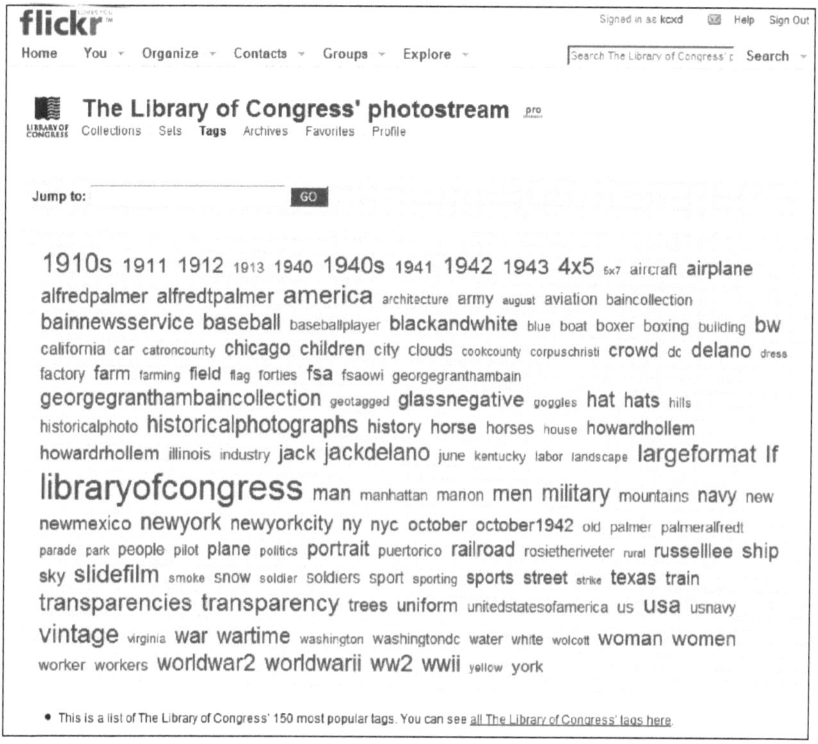

fill in information like where a picture was taken or who was pictured increases exponentially. By tapping into the enormous pool of collective wisdom of millions of Flickr users, the Library of Congress has used the community's knowledge to enhance its own bibliographic records.

Library of Congress librarian Matt Raymond notes:

> From the Library's perspective, this pilot project is a statement about the power of the web and user communities to help people better acquire information, knowledge, and most importantly wisdom. One of our goals, frankly, is to learn as much as we can about that power simply through the process of making constructive use of it.[1]

BookSpace

Built by a team of librarians, Hennepin County Library's BookSpace (www.hclib.org/pub/bookspace/) debuted in February 2007 and provided library patrons with the opportunity to build their own booklists and post comments on individual titles (Figure 4.3).

Patrons signing up for BookSpace go through a brief registration process to create their individual profiles. While the registration form includes a field for their library card number, it's an optional field – so it is possible to register and post comments even if you're not a member of HCL. Once registered, users can specify how much information they wish to make available on the public site, and have the option of including a profile picture. It's interesting to note that a high proportion of users have photos that do appear to be pictures of themselves, indicating that the library is perceived as an virtual space where it's safe to use your real identity rather than creating a purely online persona.

Figure 4.3 BookSpace

Once registered, 'My BookSpace' offers the option to create lists, comment on individual titles, share content with other users and sign up for e-mail or text message alerts when the library orders new or replacement titles by a particular author (Figure 4.4).

Adding new titles to a list or finding a title to comment on is quick and easy, requiring just a basic catalogue search and a couple of clicks. A feed on the right-hand side of the page allows easy browsing of booklists recently created by other users. Not every element of the browsing and serendipitous discovery functionality is quite as smooth as it could be; for example, the 'Related Lists' feature which appears in the right-hand column when browsing individual items is somewhat hit and miss (as I found when trying to rediscover a list that I had noted as a good example for this book) and the 'This book also belongs to...' listing is not

Figure 4.4 My BookSpace

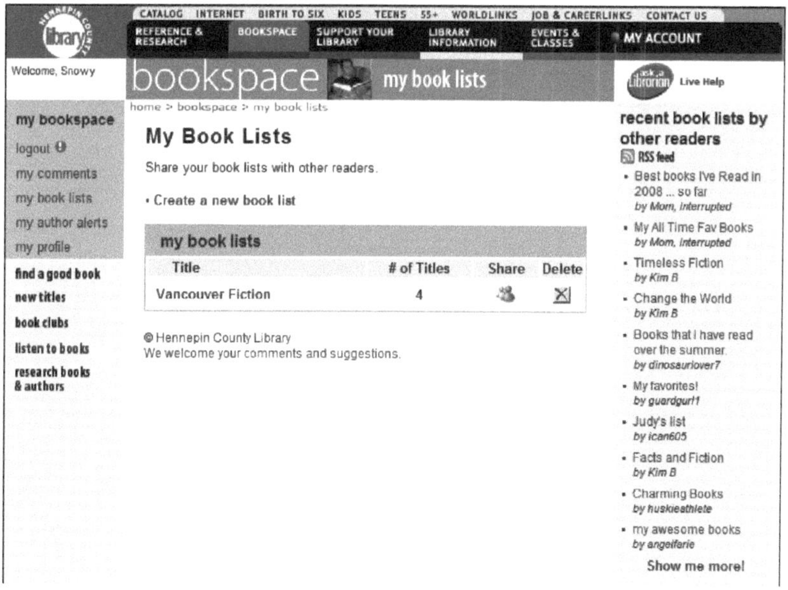

comprehensive. However, readers are provided with some basic information about the book's plot and characters, the option to browse similar subject headings within the catalogue, and a list of recent comments posted by other users (Figure 4.5). The commenting function has been fully

Figure 4.5 Individual title comments, with browsing options to the right

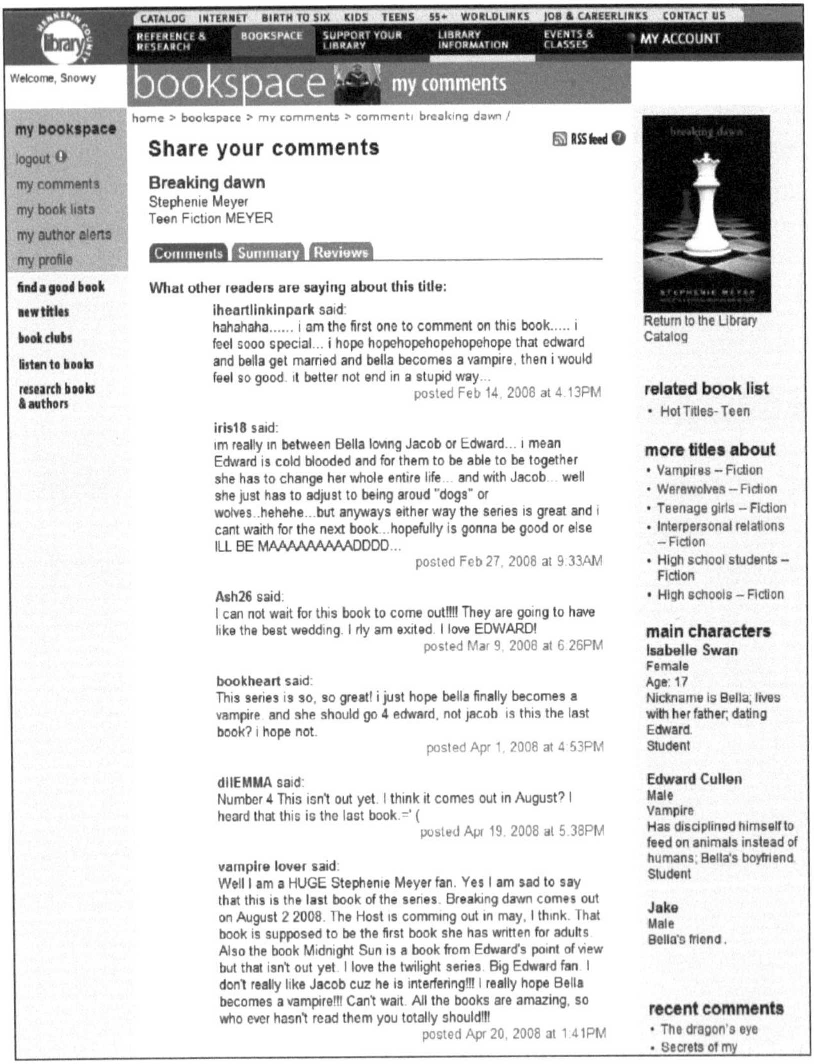

integrated with the catalogue so that patrons can see how many comments a title has while they're browsing (Figure 4.6).

BookSpace also integrates with external sites like Amazon and Barnes & Noble, providing users with the opportunity to read external reviews and purchase items they particularly like.

BookSpace is an exciting tool because it represents one of the first successful attempts to integrate user activity into the library catalogue. In the year since its launch it has certainly found a niche with Hennepin readers, with popular titles often receiving comments well into the double figures. Teen users are very active, as can be seen from a sample search of the 'Top Teens' booklist: the first five titles on the list have amassed over 150 comments between them. Browsing heavily commented items illustrates a real mix of reviews, synopses and even evolving discussions among readers. Aside from a standard disclaimer that the library is not

Figure 4.6 Catalogue entry showing the number of comments received

responsible for content contributed by readers, HCL doesn't restrict the kind of content considered appropriate for comments, creating an open and social atmosphere.

BookSpace currently seems to be strongly focused on the creation of booklists and addition of comments, although there is certainly the potential for it to evolve into more of a seamless social, discovery and readers' advisory tool. At the moment it lacks strong connections between related booklists and items; although it offers readers' advisory features like the 'Author read-a-like' search option in its 'Find a Good Book' section, this has been separated from the general search functions and consequently doesn't integrate smoothly as a discovery tool. Nonetheless, BookSpace represents not just an innovative new direction for the library catalogue and website, but also proof that when it comes to ways for libraries to engage their users online, if you build it then they will, in fact, come.

Chinese Canadian Genealogy wiki

The Chinese Canadian Genealogy wiki (http://ccgwiki.vpl.ca/) is the result of a collaboration between Vancouver Public Library and Library and Archives Canada. Using the wiki module of the Expression Engine content management system that powers the library's website, VPL has built a wiki which contains 461 profiles based on the first 461 entries in the Chinese Immigration List (Figure 4.7). (Under the Chinese Immigration Act of 1923, the basic details of all individuals born in Canada of Chinese origin were recorded in this list.)

The details as taken from the list are sparse, and in many cases there are few other records of the lives of the individuals named in the profiles. The wiki is unique in that

Figure 4.7 The Chinese Canadian Genealogy wiki – profiles from a community

it provides space for those who knew these individuals – friends, family members, descendants, researchers – to fill in the blanks, not only with missing vital statistics but with the stories of their lives. In this way the wiki aims to evolve from a static list of basic details to a rich, living picture of individuals and communities.

Users need to register and agree to the library's terms of service to be able to update the wiki. Once registered, a simple click is all that's required to open the editing interface for a page.

The CCG wiki is a great example of the value that can be added when a library enters into a true collaboration with the community. The wiki combines the research expertise of librarians, who compiled and organized the original data from the Immigration List into profiles, and the personal knowledge and experiences of individual members of the community. By acknowledging the value in that personal knowledge, and seeking it out and marrying it with the hard data from the Immigration List, the library has created a far richer and more well-rounded picture of the lives of 461 Chinese-Canadian individuals than would have been possible through its research alone.

Evolver

Evolver is the somewhat garish teen site of Denver Public Library (http://teens.denverlibrary.org/involved/index.html), which actively encourages teens to 'get involved' as one of the main menu options (Figure 4.8).

One of Evolver's best features is the space it provides for content contributed by teens. 'Write a review' allows teens to write reviews and submit them to DPL, although this is not the kind of synchronous posting available on

Figure 4.8 Evolver

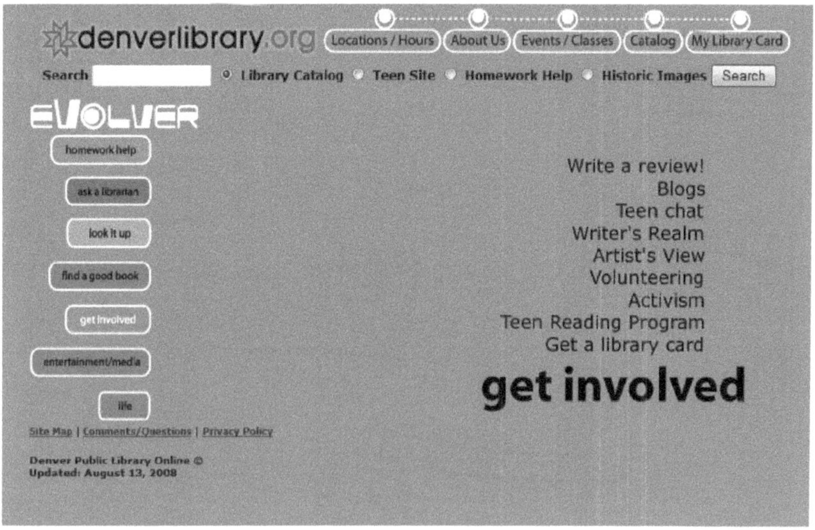

Source: http://teens.denverlibrary.org/involved/index.html

BookSpace: reviews are read and edited by librarians before being posted in a separate section of the site. The 'Writer's Realm' section also invites teens to submit original writing, ranging from creative writing to poetry, comics and rap lyrics. Uptake of this feature seems to have been relatively limited – just two pieces of original work are currently on display – which may be due to a rather laborious submission process that involves sending the library a print copy of a release form, along with a print or e-mail copy of the piece of writing for publication.

DPL has also used Evolver to extend its web presence beyond its own site, into other online spaces. The 'Artist's View' section links to the library's Flickr page, where artwork submitted by teens in response to competitions is hosted, along with many user photographs of library events for teens. An embedded Flickr widget also displays the latest content on the original DPL page (Figure 4.9).

Figure 4.9 Evolver – Artist's View

Source: http://teens.denverlibrary.org/involved/view_links.html

Evolver maintains an active MySpace profile where librarians blog about teen news and events, encourage teens to participate in library surveys and link back to teen-contributed content on the main Evolver page (Figure 4.10). Embedded Shelfari and Flickr widgets are used to promote books and artwork, and there are buttons leading to the

Figure 4.10 The Evolver MySpace page

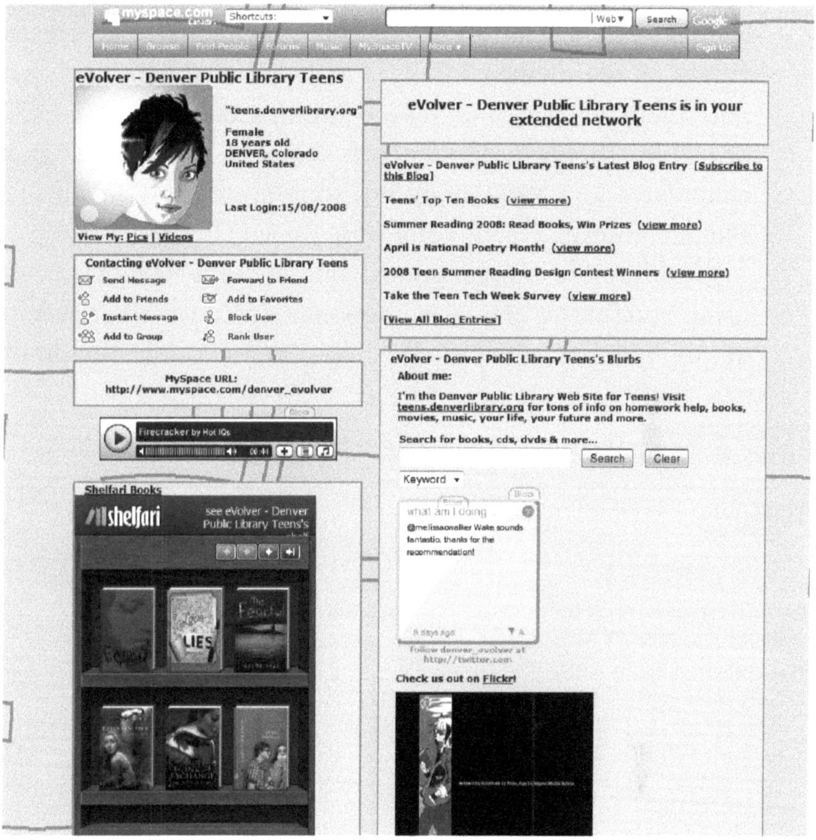

Source: www.myspace.com/denver_evolver

library's subscription databases and the AskColorado virtual reference services. At the time of writing the Evolver MySpace profile has 793 friends, predominantly teens from the Denver area, and 166 current comments. It would be interesting to know the activity levels on the MySpace page to determine how they compare to interest on the main DPL webpage: are teens more likely to contribute in the less formal, more familiar setting of MySpace?

DPL has also used YouTube as an innovative way of engaging teens with its services. The Evolver YouTube competition, which ran in fall 2007, invited teens to create videos on the theme of 'How I have fun at the library' and post them to YouTube. The winning video, which is still available, shows a number of shots of the library and culminates in a very funny rap song about how much the filmmaker loves Harry Potter (Figure 4.11).

In addition to content contributed by teens, DPL has been using YouTube to create promotional videos for other events at the library, including 'The Summer of Reading'

Figure 4.11 The winning video from Evolver's YouTube contest

Source: www.youtube.com/watch?v=W9aHMj2VWJk

(www.youtube.com/watch?v=5AppCIzJD84), where the DPL kitty decides he'd rather be reading and playing Dance Dance Revolution at the library than working for the summer; 'The You Know What' (www.youtube.com/watch?v=QJ104WNMWaU); and 'The Super War' (www.youtube.com/watch?v=7u7h8AGC78Y), created and produced by attendees at the library's 'After School is Cool' children's technology workshop.

Uptake on the YouTube videos is relatively low key when compared to the millions of hits received by some of the site's best-known videos, but is noteworthy considering the size of the library-going Denver teen community. The winning Evolver video, which was part of a contest that only ran for a short time, has received close to 1,000 views and ten comments, and has been made a favorite by six people.

Evolver is a great example of the mash-up versus build-up principle: how widgets and content from other sites can be used to enhance a library's webpage and bring its site to life.

Book Buzz

Toronto Public Library runs Book Buzz (http://bookbuzz.torontopubliclibrary.ca/), a virtual book club open to anyone interested in joining in a discussion about reading (Figure 4.12).

A new title is selected each month by the librarian, and an accompanying discussion is launched in the Book Buzz forum. TPL complements the discussion by bringing authors of selected monthly titles in for live chat sessions approximately twice per year.

Registering for Book Buzz is quick and easy: users are presented with a short list of rules, which essentially add up

Figure 4.12 Book Buzz, the TPL discussion group

to agreeing to behave respectfully and not post illegal or commercial content, provide their e-mail address and choose a user name and password. A library card is not required.

The Book Buzz discussion forum offers a number of discussions: the current book of the month, contests and open topics about reading. The Book Buzz community generate steady discussion; a brief browse through previous book of the month discussions reveals an average of between 50 and 100 posts per book.

Browsing through the discussions reveals a small, loyal community who love talking about books and are keen to share their knowledge and tips (Figure 4.13). The 'Ask a Bookhead' discussion has more than 200 posts, most of which are responses to requests for recommendations. Discussion is consistently good-natured and frequently includes friendly asides about the offline lives of people posting – for example, how they're going to try to make time in a busy schedule to read the latest book of the month, or

Figure 4.13 Open discussions, showing number of posts

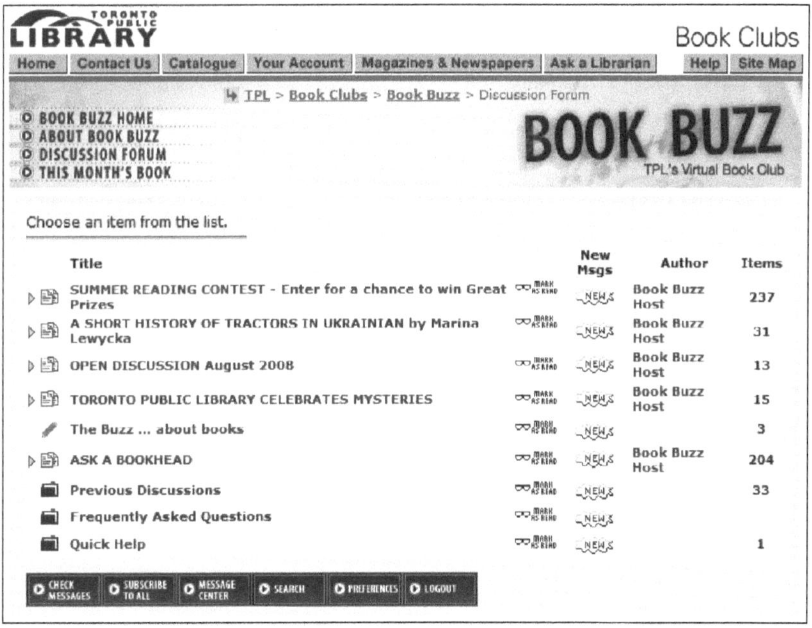

Source: http://bookbuzzdiscussion.torontopubliclibrary.ca/webx?14@155.hiwea05NeF7.25@.bebc200

personal recollections based on themes or incidents in the book. Although TPL discourages users from registering with their real names, a number have done so anyway; this may be an indication that they consider Book Buzz a 'safe' online space. Certainly the community appear to know one another well, and very much enjoy the participatory nature of the book club. Book Buzz member Vicki comments from her vacation on 8 August that she has 'Just logged in from the Halifax Public Library public computer system for my Book Buzz fix...'

The Book Buzz host, a librarian (or librarians?) from TPL, plays an active part in the discussion, encouraging debate and offering themes and suggestions to stimulate the conversation.

The Book Buzz interface is simple, although not the easiest to navigate for a brand-new user; navigating through a lengthy discussion with many posts is more laborious than it should be, and preference changes (at least during my tests of the site) don't always stick. But it's very easy to post a message or reply to another user's comment, and that seems to be more than enough to encourage enthusiastic readers to participate.

CPL's WordPress teen blog

Cheshire Public Library (Connecticut) has used the WordPress hosted publishing platform to set up a blog where library teens can share book reviews and comments (http://cpltbb.wordpress.com/).

The blog allows teens to register, post reviews and comment on reviews shared by other people. The blog entries' categorization function has been used to create a detailed genre list, enabling quick and easy searching of reviews by genre. The use of cover images is a nice touch adding visual appeal to the blog (Figure 4.14).

Figure 4.14 The Cheshire Public Library teen book blog

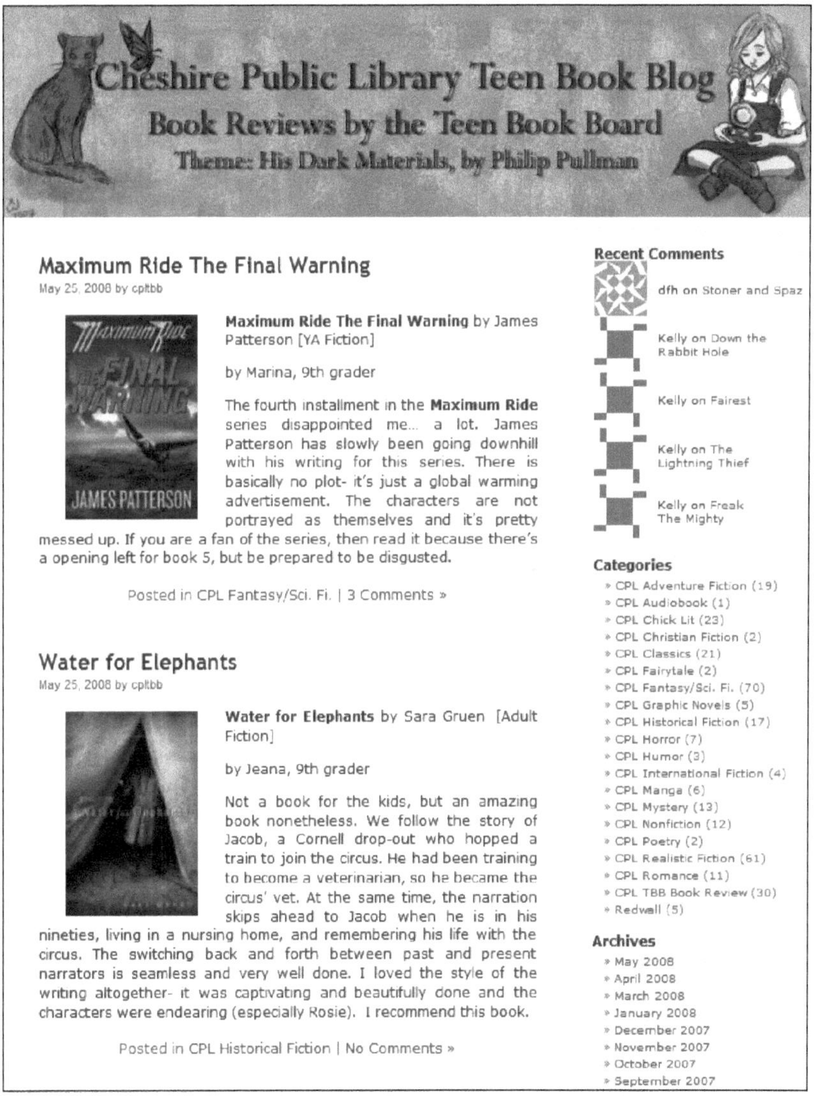

Cheshire Public Library Teen Book Blog
Book Reviews by the Teen Book Board
Theme: His Dark Materials, by Philip Pullman

Maximum Ride The Final Warning

May 25, 2008 by cpltbb

Maximum Ride The Final Warning by James Patterson [YA Fiction]

by Marina, 9th grader

The fourth installment in the **Maximum Ride** series disappointed me... a lot. James Patterson has slowly been going downhill with his writing for this series. There is basically no plot- it's just a global warming advertisement. The characters are not portrayed as themselves and it's pretty messed up. If you are a fan of the series, then read it because there's a opening left for book 5, but be prepared to be disgusted.

Posted in CPL Fantasy/Sci. Fi. | 3 Comments »

Water for Elephants

May 25, 2008 by cpltbb

Water for Elephants by Sara Gruen [Adult Fiction]

by Jeana, 9th grader

Not a book for the kids, but an amazing book nonetheless. We follow the story of Jacob, a Cornell drop-out who hopped a train to join the circus. He had been training to become a veterinarian, so he became the circus' vet. At the same time, the narration skips ahead to Jacob when he is in his nineties, living in a nursing home, and remembering his life with the circus. The switching back and forth between past and present narrators is seamless and very well done. I loved the style of the writing altogether- it was captivating and beautifully done and the characters were endearing (especially Rosie). I recommend this book.

Posted in CPL Historical Fiction | No Comments »

Recent Comments

dfh on Stoner and Spaz
Kelly on Down the Rabbit Hole
Kelly on Fairest
Kelly on The Lightning Thief
Kelly on Freak The Mighty

Categories

- CPL Adventure Fiction (19)
- CPL Audiobook (1)
- CPL Chick Lit (23)
- CPL Christian Fiction (2)
- CPL Classics (21)
- CPL Fairytale (2)
- CPL Fantasy/Sci. Fi. (70)
- CPL Graphic Novels (5)
- CPL Historical Fiction (17)
- CPL Horror (7)
- CPL Humor (3)
- CPL International Fiction (4)
- CPL Manga (6)
- CPL Mystery (13)
- CPL Nonfiction (12)
- CPL Poetry (2)
- CPL Realistic Fiction (61)
- CPL Romance (11)
- CPL TBB Book Review (30)
- Redwall (5)

Archives

- May 2008
- April 2008
- March 2008
- January 2008
- December 2007
- November 2007
- October 2007
- September 2007

Source: http://cpltbb.wordpress.com/

The blog appears to have a relatively small, steady following, with a couple of new reviews posted per month and most reviews receiving two or three comments.

Twittering libraries

Microblogging site Twitter is a great resource for libraries to share news and updates, inform users about new resources, promote current events and training courses and even share newly added catalogue items (Figures 4.15–4.17).

Figure 4.15 Cleveland Public Library

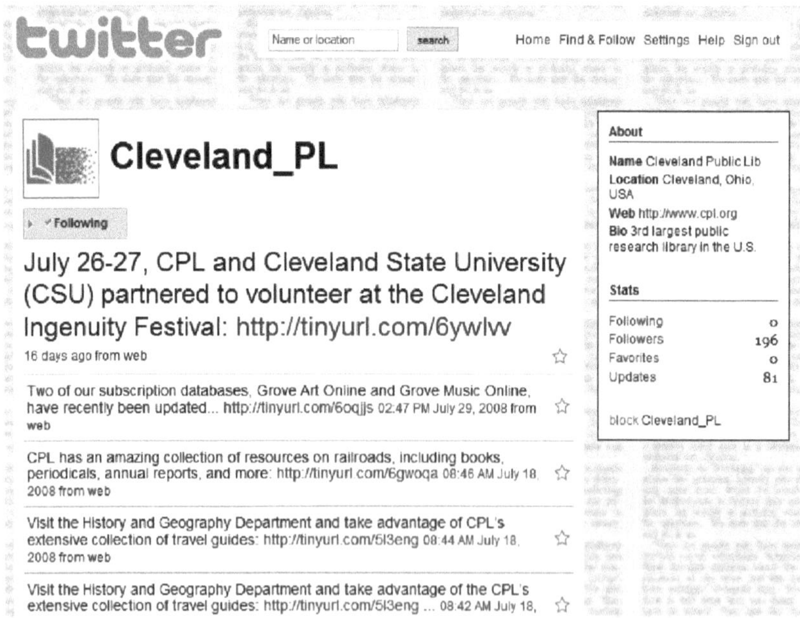

Source: http://twitter.com/Cleveland_PL

Figure 4.16 Casa Grande Public Library

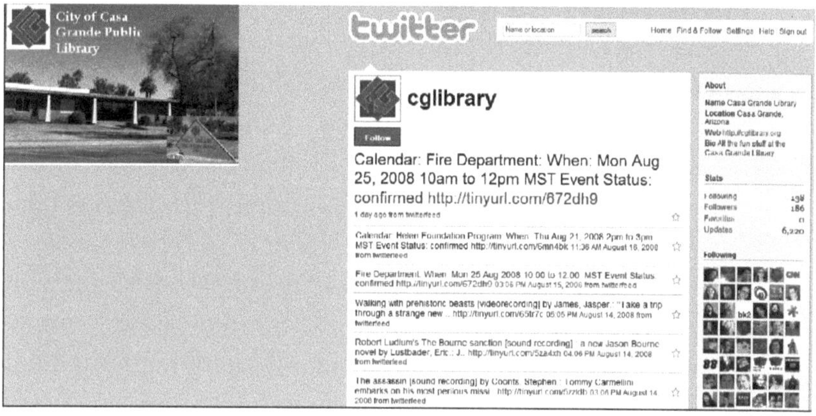

Source: http://twitter.com/cglibrary

Figure 4.17 Henry County Library

Source: http://twitter.com/hcpl

Build up versus mash up: BiblioCommons

These tools are all very cool, but one thing the majority have in common is that they're quite random and are being implemented piecemeal within library sites. One library might have a blog, LibraryThing catalogue integration and a Facebook page; another might have YouTube videos, a Delicious.com link collection and an online book club run on a PHP bulletin board. Overall, the philosophy among libraries seems to be very much to mash up rather than build up: to take existing tools and integrate them into the library website rather than creating their own tools. This makes sense, especially where resources are scarce and libraries want to minimize the workload involved in implementation. However, although Web 2.0 applications can be used to great effect in the library world, they were generally not created specifically with libraries in mind. Which leads to the question: what might we accomplish if we took this technology and built something that specifically addresses the items our users have told us they would most like to see in our websites? The answer is BiblioCommons.

BiblioCommons (www.bibliocommons.com) promises to be a very exciting addition to the library world. Started by entrepreneur Beth Jefferson in 2004, this 12-person company is set to revolutionize not only the faithful library catalogue, but also the way it integrates with other web services. BiblioCommons is essentially a social discovery layer that sits on top of the iPac, replacing all existing iPac functionality and allowing users to search, rate titles, build lists, make recommendations, tag, post comments and share all of this content with other library users. It incorporates many of the best elements of Hennepin's BookSpace, but includes a wide range of additional features – tagging, rating and the ability to build a network of trusted users – and adopts a more seamless approach between the different discovery elements.

The first BiblioCommons installation recently went live at Oakville Public Library, a small city (population 160,000) in Ontario, giving curious users a first chance to explore this reinvented iPac (www.opl.on.ca/). The results are, to say the least, impressive.

The first thing you notice (or perhaps it would be more accurate to say, don't notice) is the complete integration of the website and catalogue. It's so seamless and smooth that there is literally no way for the end user to tell where one ends and the other begins.

The commitment to discovery is inherent in OPL's primary navigation bar, which invites users to 'Explore'. Choosing this option leads to a page where BiblioCommons widgets display browsable bookshelves of newly acquired and recently returned items (Figure 4.18), creating the virtual equivalent of the returns shelving truck that always seems to hold such fascination for patrons who come into the library without a clear idea of what they'd like to borrow.

These widgets are both visually attractive and useful, and Jefferson acknowledges that they were where the bulk of the social activity and participation occurred during beta testing.[2] However, there are already plans to expand widget functionality to allow libraries direct control of widget content. Possible uses include highlighting items that are about to be discarded, creating a promotional tool for underused items and giving patrons a last chance to borrow them before they leave the library's shelves for good; creating collections for specific calendar days or events, for example Pride Week, the Olympics or Canada Day; highlighting local authors; and promoting library events such as poetry readings.[3]

Figure 4.18 Exploring Oakville Public Library

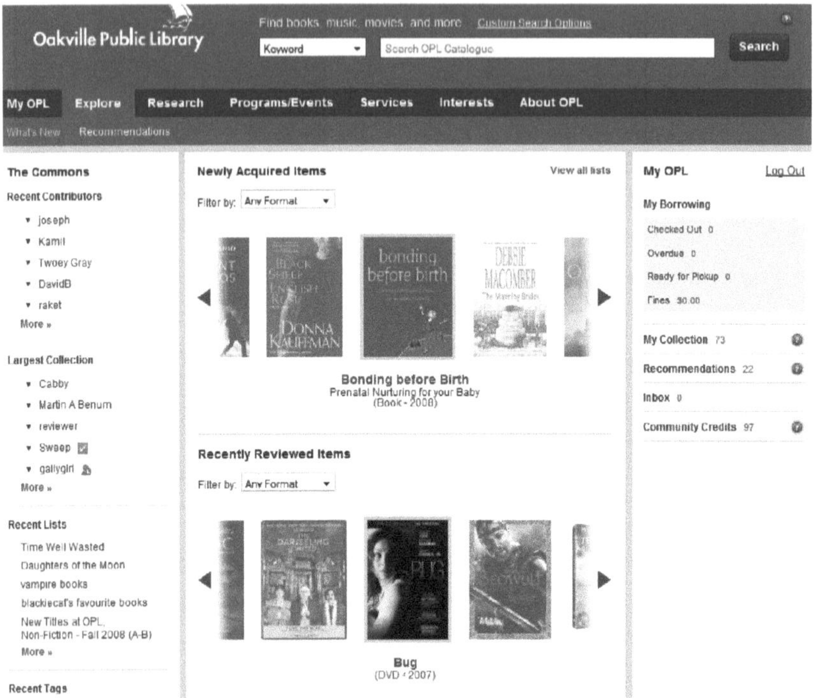

On the left side of the page, the social layer of the catalogue is immediately highlighted. 'The Commons' provides lists of users who have recently been active on the site; those with the largest collections; new booklists (which may have been created by patrons or library staff); and recent item tags.

To begin participating, library patrons need to sign in and then visit 'My OPL' (Figure 4.19). Initial registration requires a library card, but after this step is complete all that are needed for subsequent sign-ins are a user-selected login name and password. The library card ensures that while the experience provides users with anonymity when interacting with each other, accountability is built into the system: user activity can be connected back to the individual library card

Figure 4.19 My OPL

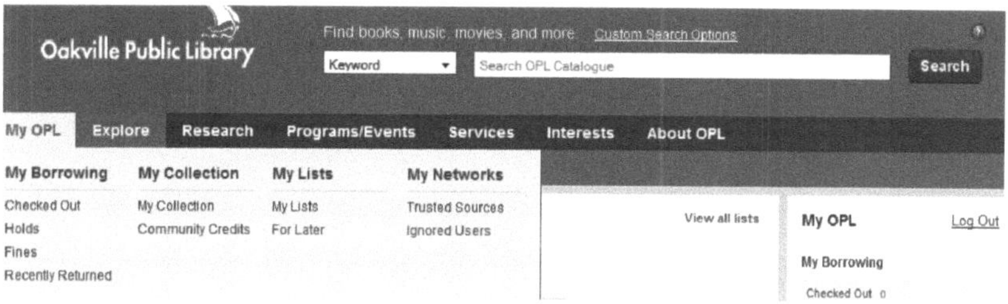

used for registration. This makes it likely that the 'ultimate catalogue' (as OPL describes the BiblioCommons experience) will not be plagued by the kinds of flamewars and trolling that often proliferate on open discussion forums.

My OPL integrates traditional 'account' functionality – access to renewals, holds and fines – with BiblioCommons's unique social discovery layer. Users can build lists of titles, or even rebuild their entire collection online using the library catalogue. Individual items can be commented on, rated from one to five stars and flagged for age suitability, violence and bad language (Figure 4.20). All actions that users perform can be shared with other registered users, or kept private.

One of the neatest things about BiblioCommons is the implementation of user tagging. Tags fall into three categories: genre, tone and theme. By providing this basic level of guidance, the system encourages the user to build a rich folksonomy that allows others to browse easily through related items. To facilitate serendipitous discovery, BiblioCommons also allows users to add titles that they have found to be similar to the item. Tags, lists to which an item belongs, similar titles and the traditional iPac subject headings all appear in the left-hand column as the user browses the site, along with a 'Browse the shelf' option that

Figure 4.20 Individual book entry, showing possible actions

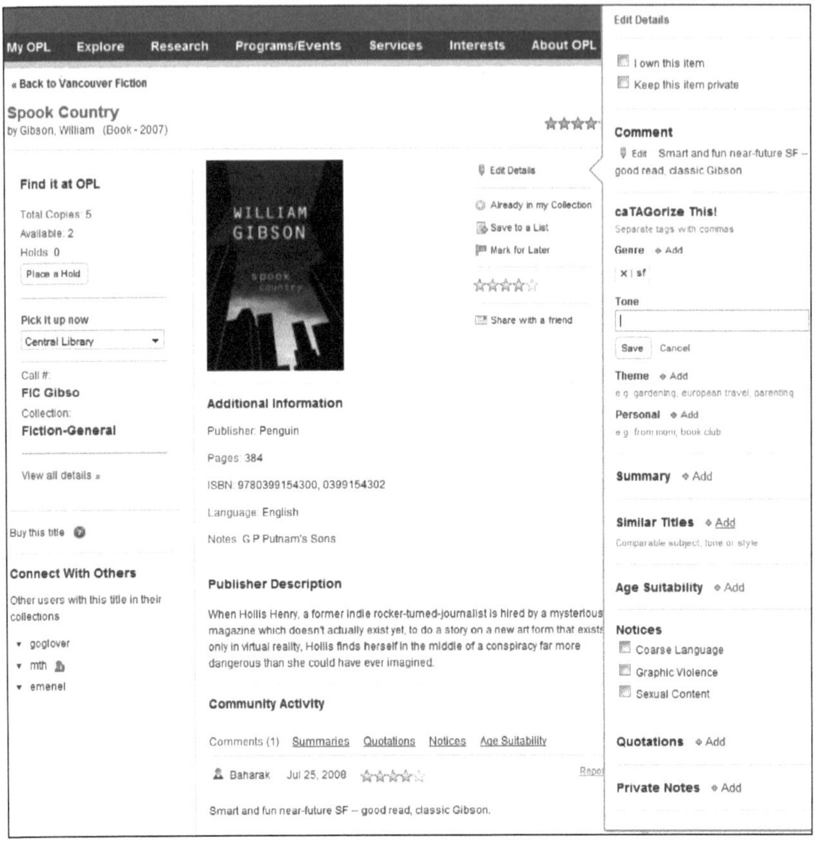

launches a widget showing other items in this area of the library's collection (Figure 4.21).

To encourage participation, BiblioCommons also offers a unique system of community credits. These reward users for each book rated, comment posted, item tagged or other action on the site. As the test site, OPL is offering the fairly substantial reward of a trip to any public library in Canada to the patron who builds up the most credits, but going forward libraries may choose to redeem these for money off fines or additional free holds.

Figure 4.21 Browsing the shelf

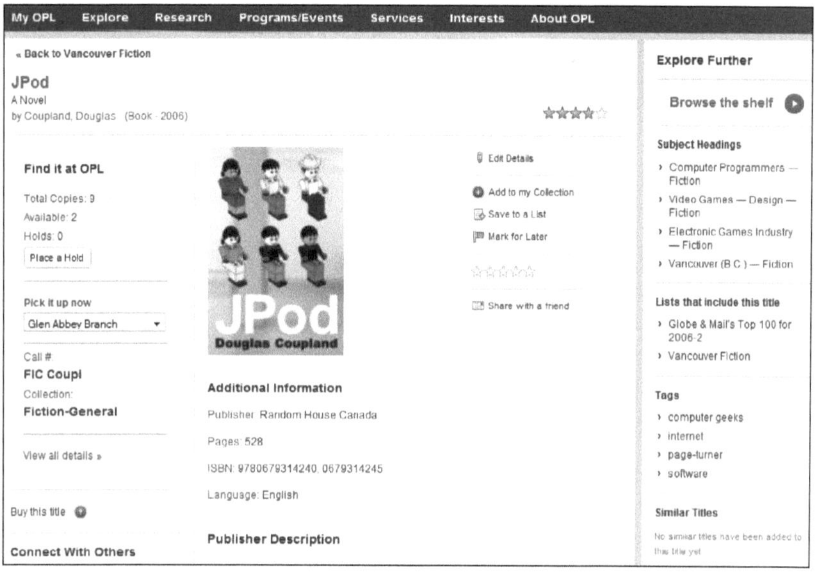

BiblioCommons has not stinted on the search functionality. Jefferson acknowledges that a substantial amount of development effort has been focused on the search, and it's interesting to compare the results to the kind of response the same search would get from a traditional iPac.

The basic search options are far simpler than the typical list of iPac indexes: keyword, author, title, subject and tag. The tag search is quite unique in that it allows users to browse tags that other people have given items, giving an extra layer of credibility and purpose to the user-generated folksonomy. The subject search is also unique in that, as the user types, it brings up a list of suggested subject headings from the catalogue (Figure 4.22) – finding a neat balance between the precision of the legacy catalogue and the flexibility and smart searching of Google.

Figure 4.22 Catalogue search with suggested subject headings

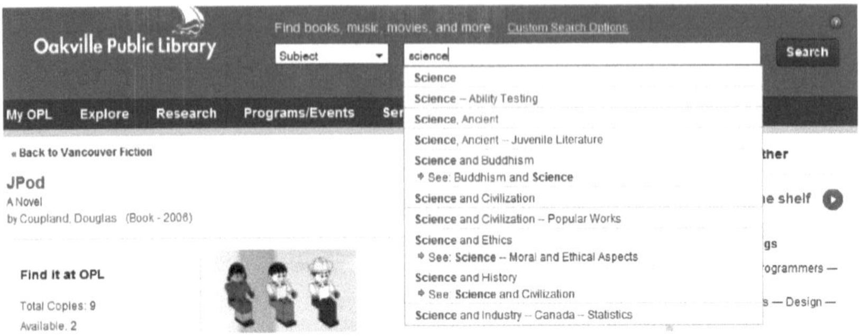

The keyword search is also more intelligent than the typical iPac search. Its algorithms accord more weight to complete titles, and the ranking of results lists is correspondingly more relevant and useful.

One interesting aspect of BiblioCommons is that it does not market itself as a social networking tool, but rather a discovery tool. Although users do have the option to send private messages to each other, the only real networking opportunity is a small flag that they can use to identify 'trusted' users. (This flag is subject-specific, so it's possible to trust a user in certain subject areas but not in others – for example, you might choose to trust someone's travel writing recommendations but not their taste in fiction.) The focus is all about building content that will connect people with books, DVDs and other catalogue items rather than other users, while still relying on people's natural curiosity about each other to drive interest and participation.

BiblioCommons is unique because rather than taking Web 2.0 tools and incorporating them into library web services, it has taken Web 2.0 technologies and created a tool specifically for libraries. It has taken our legacy application – the catalogue – and turned it into the kind of dynamic, participative, interactive discovery tool that allows users to create content, inform each other and ultimately receive a better level of service that also encourages their engagement and involvement with the library. BiblioCommons is by no means perfect, but the early implementation is impressive and it offers a very interesting new direction for libraries and the services they deliver online.

Mash up versus build up: Vancouver Public Library

Following the launch of a new website in February 2008, Vancouver Public Library has been keen to explore the potential of social networking and participatory tools. We have tried to be very strategic about our implementation of these tools, piloting items that we feel will truly enhance library services. In terms of content delivered via our own website, we have very much espoused the philosophy of mash up versus build up: taking advantage of the tools that already exist rather than reinventing the wheel. Our site includes embedded YouTube videos, Flickr photographs, RSS feeds and branch blogs.

In addition, we have been keen to explore the potential of expanding the library's online presence beyond our own web space. Again, we have tried to be strategic and look for tools where there is a real opportunity for either community engagement or enhancement of the way we deliver information to our users. One of the biggest challenges on the modern web is identifying exactly which of the myriad tools, technologies and new software products can really add value for our patrons, and which of the plethora of social networking sites provide a genuine platform for opening a dialogue with users.

While our adoption of Web 2.0 tools within the VPL website was largely based on traditional feedback mechanisms like user surveys, focus groups and patron interviews, we took a slightly different approach to identifying social networking opportunities. When VPL began looking at the possibility of stepping outside of its own web space, we conducted a series of searches to see if the library was already a topic of conversation on the social web. We hoped that the results would help us target these early promotional and engagement efforts towards sites where they would be most effective.

Twitter

Using the Summize search (which has since been purchased by Twitter and is available at http://search.twitter.com), we ran a brief test in May 2008 and found that Vancouver area Twitterers were already engaged in active discussion about library services, facilities and events – not to mention numerous comments (some flattering, some less so) about the landmark Central Library building (Figure 4.23).

Given that the library was already a topic of some interest on Twitter, we launched a pilot VPL Twitter account. To date we have used it to share service updates, library news and regular bulletins about library programs, events and training courses (Figure 4.24).

A brief period of test-posting content to Twitter resulted in 75 followers, even with no active promotion of the page. We have found that the microblogging format lends itself really well to short, quick updates highlighting service news and library events. Initial feedback from the Twitter community, which has been easy to track thanks to the Twitter search tool, has also been positive (Figure 4.25).

Figure 4.23 Twitter search results for Vancouver Public Library

Source: http://search.twitter.com/search?q=vancouver+public+library

Figure 4.24 VPL's Twitter feed

Source: http://twitter.com/VPL

Figure 4.25 A local Twitter user tweets about our updates

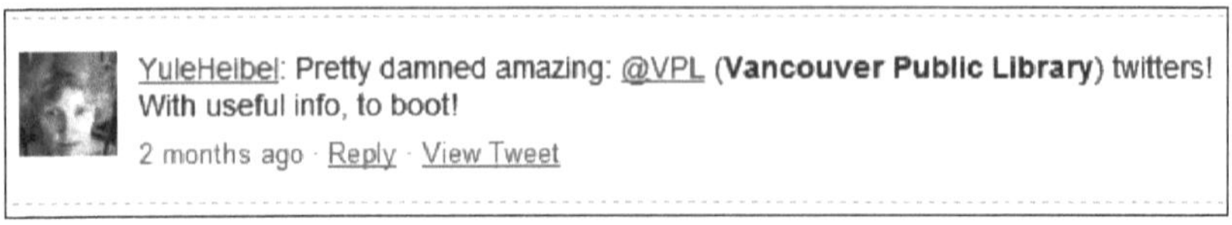

Of course, with success comes the need to turn a pilot project into an ongoing operation. Our goal now is to ensure regular content updates, and formal promotion of the Twitter account via our own website.

Facebook

Facebook is another site with strong local ties, as its networks are built partly around geographic areas. It also has an extremely strong librarian community – particularly those librarians with an interest in technology and Web 2.0 applications – and local library interest, with groups already existing for VPL Facebookers and British Columbia's virtual reference service, AskAway. With such a strong overall online presence, a large local network base – the Vancouver area network has close to 800,000 members – and a library-centric community to help with promotion, Facebook was another obvious choice; especially as, along with MySpace, Facebook has become a ubiquitous presence in the social networking world.

Unlike MySpace, Facebook only allows profiles to be created for people. To create a Facebook presence for an organization, a page has to be created. Users can then choose to subscribe to the page and become fans of the organization. Pages combine a number of features from Facebook's group and individual profiles: a wall where anyone can post, a discussion area for debate on specific topics and the ability to upload video and photographs. It also includes promotional tools such as fee-based advertising, the ability to broadcast a message to all fans and usage statistics. The page must be created by one individual, but others can then be invited to join as administrators.

We have used VPL's page to highlight occasional library events, upload a video introducing the library's new website and add photographs (Figure 4.26). Again, the page has

Figure 4.26 VPL's Facebook page

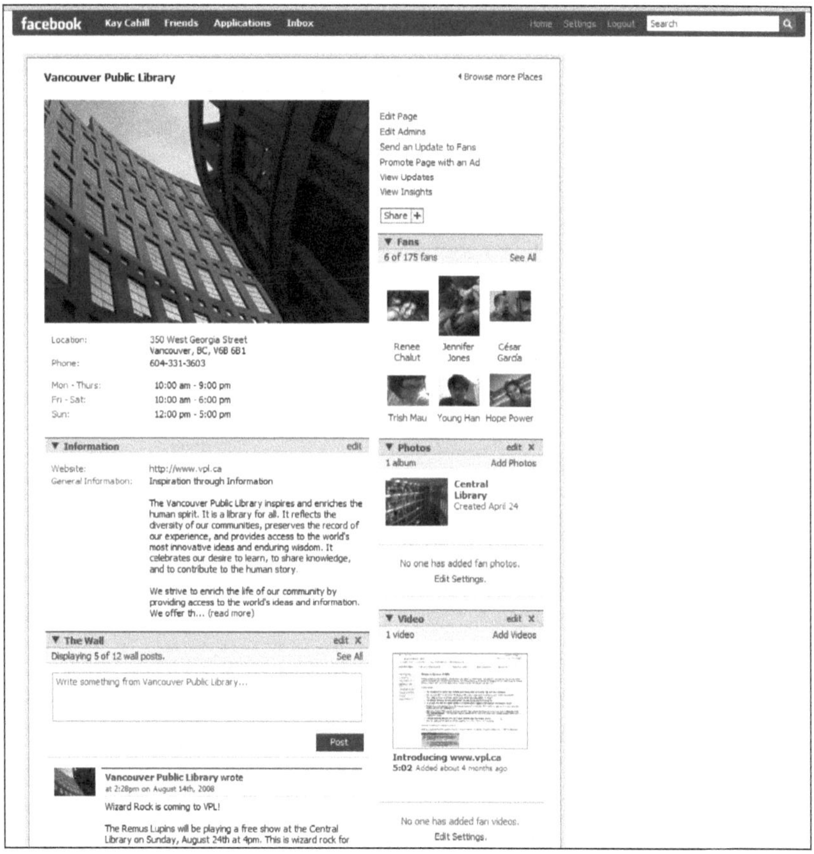

Source: www.new.facebook.com/pages/Vancouver-BC/Vancouver-Public-Library/15388201565

received relatively little formal promotion, but has acquired 284 fans at the time of writing (not all of them librarians!) and has a steady trickle of new fans joining each week. The in-built statistics package shows that since the page was created, it has received an average of five views per day.

One of the neatest things about VPL's Facebook page is watching the unsolicited wall posts roll in from patrons, mixed in with formal updates from the library (Figure 4.27). These have been quite random in nature, and have so far been predominantly positive. The library has also posted a couple of test discussions to see if the Facebook discussion board is a good venue to solicit user feedback about library services.

VPL has also been experimenting with Facebook applications. Widgetbox (www.widgetbox.com) is a site that enables users to create web widgets with information as simple as a blog URL or RSS feed. By running the VPL News RSS feed through Widgetbox, we generated a widget that could then be easily turned into an application for embedding on Facebook profiles (Figure 4.28).

Potentially, any piece of information on the VPL site that can be converted into a widget – our branch blogs, events archive or any of our new titles lists – could then be converted into a Facebook app in this way. One of the advantages of using Widgetbox as an intermediary is that no specialized programming or technical knowledge is required to create the widgets. This makes it very quick and easy to create new apps and offer them on Facebook, giving us a chance to see what kind of demand there is for this kind of library-related content among the Facebook community. With technical support, even our catalogue quick-search box could be converted to an application for users to embed in their profiles. Because of the increased development time, we would look for evidence that users would appreciate and

Figure 4.27 VPL Facebook wall posts

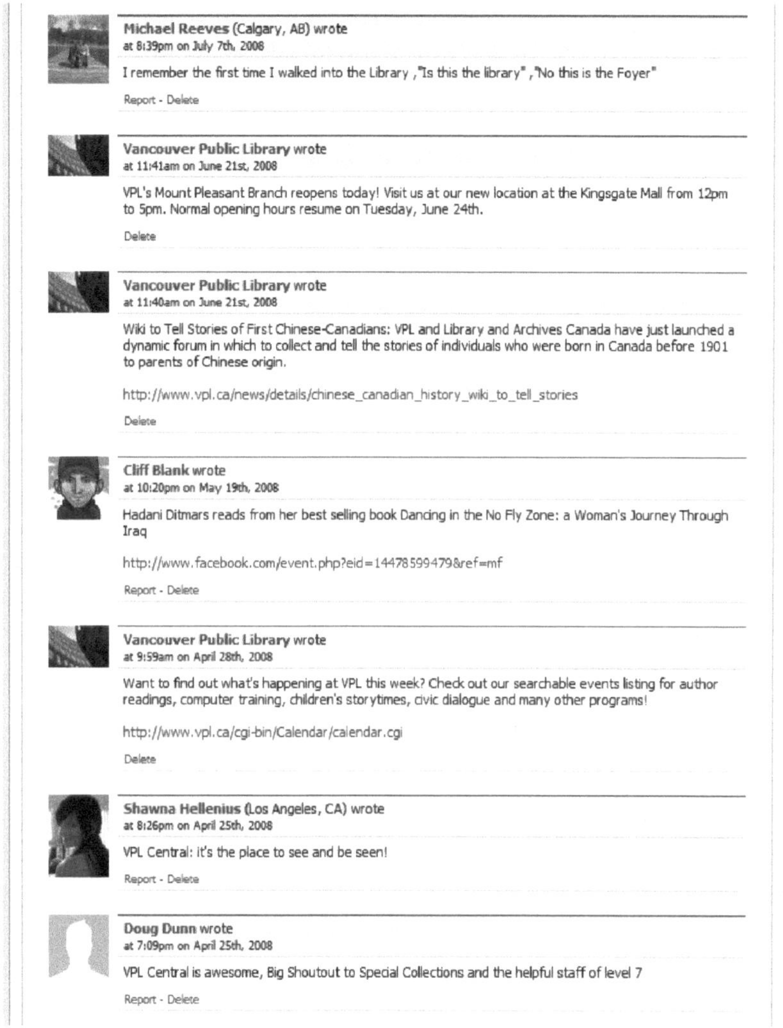

Michael Reeves (Calgary, AB) wrote
at 8:39pm on July 7th, 2008
I remember the first time I walked into the Library ,"Is this the library" ,"No this is the Foyer"
Report - Delete

Vancouver Public Library wrote
at 11:41am on June 21st, 2008
VPL's Mount Pleasant Branch reopens today! Visit us at our new location at the Kingsgate Mall from 12pm to 5pm. Normal opening hours resume on Tuesday, June 24th.
Delete

Vancouver Public Library wrote
at 11:40am on June 21st, 2008
Wiki to Tell Stories of First Chinese-Canadians: VPL and Library and Archives Canada have just launched a dynamic forum in which to collect and tell the stories of individuals who were born in Canada before 1901 to parents of Chinese origin.
http://www.vpl.ca/news/details/chinese_canadian_history_wiki_to_tell_stories
Delete

Cliff Blank wrote
at 10:20pm on May 19th, 2008
Hadani Ditmars reads from her best selling book Dancing in the No Fly Zone: a Woman's Journey Through Iraq
http://www.facebook.com/event.php?eid=14478599479&ref=mf
Report - Delete

Vancouver Public Library wrote
at 9:59am on April 28th, 2008
Want to find out what's happening at VPL this week? Check out our searchable events listing for author readings, computer training, children's storytimes, civic dialogue and many other programs!
http://www.vpl.ca/cgi-bin/Calendar/calendar.cgi
Delete

Shawna Hellenius (Los Angeles, CA) wrote
at 8:26pm on April 25th, 2008
VPL Central: it's the place to see and be seen!
Report - Delete

Doug Dunn wrote
at 7:09pm on April 25th, 2008
VPL Central is awesome, Big Shoutout to Special Collections and the helpful staff of level 7
Report - Delete

Source: www.new.facebook.com/wall.php?id=15388201565

use this kind of application before investing significant effort in its production.

Figure 4.28 The VPL News Releases Facebook app

MySpace

Library MySpace profiles are considered fairly standard tools for building connections with teenagers. VPL has had a MySpace page for some time; it was created as a demo during one of the library's Techno Tuesday courses introducing the public to social networking tools. The page has had little work done on it since and remains fairly basic, but it does highlight key library services likely to be of interest to teens. We recently added the news feed widget to the page; this automatically posts any new items from the VPL homepage, creating new content on the MySpace page without the need for any additional work by the library (Figure 4.29). The library currently has 116 MySpace friends, including a number of other libraries.

Figure 4.29 VPL on MySpace

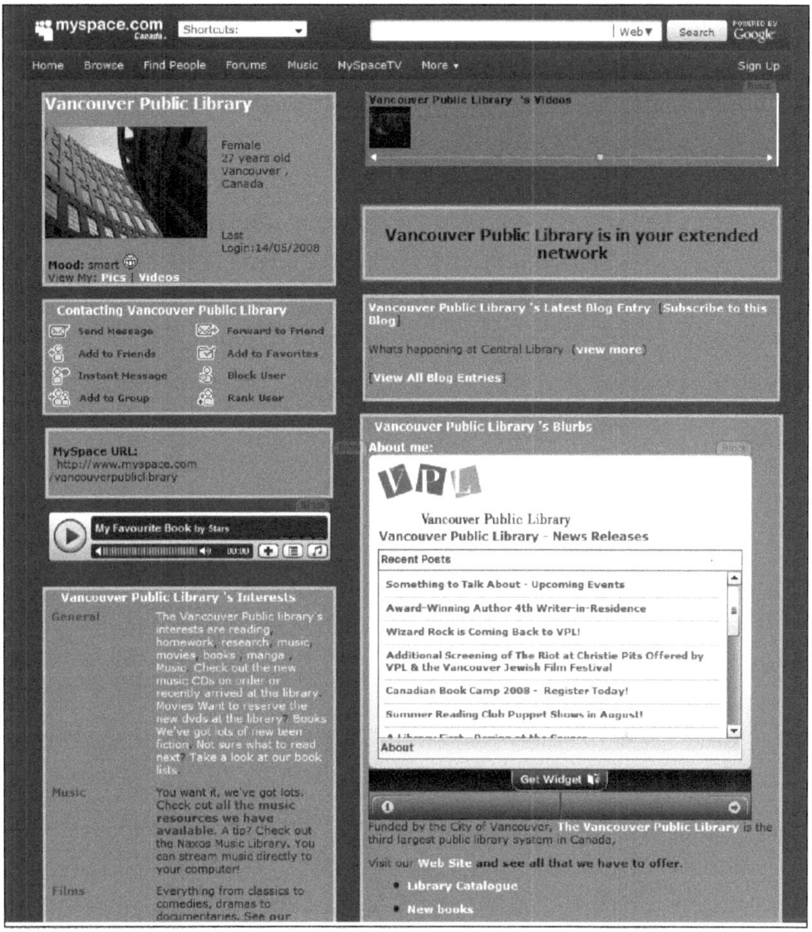

Source: www.myspace.com/vancouverpubliclibrary

Our future plans include involving the library's Teen Advisory Group in the further development of the page, ensuring that it develops in a relevant and meaningful way, and using it to promote activities and events for teens organized by the library.

YouTube

VPL's YouTube page was started to enable us to host video content and then embed it in our website. Our first YouTube videos were a series of tutorials designed to help users get to know the new library website following its launch in February 2008 (Figure 4.30). The tutorials are accessible on the main library website via a video guide, and have been viewed around 600 times since being posted. However, we also discovered that YouTube is perhaps not the ideal location for this kind of content. The quality of the uploaded videos was so much poorer than the originals that much of the smaller text on the website is unclear, and the value of the video to the end user is significantly diminished. We uploaded one of the tutorials to the library's Facebook page and found that this version retained the original quality. We are currently looking at other options – for example, Vimeo – for instructional content that relies on detailed visual images.

YouTube has proven a much more effective venue for more typical video content, like promotional footage from the recent 'Boxing @ Library Square' event, and we hope to create and upload video tours of the library's buildings and collections in the near future. These will be available both via VPL's YouTube channel and as embedded content in our own website.

Flickr

Because VPL's Central Library is such an iconic building, VPL was a hot topic on Flickr long before we started our own account. Our preliminary search found close to 4,000 photographs and 23 groups tagged with 'Vancouver Public Library'.

Figure 4.30 VPL's YouTube channel

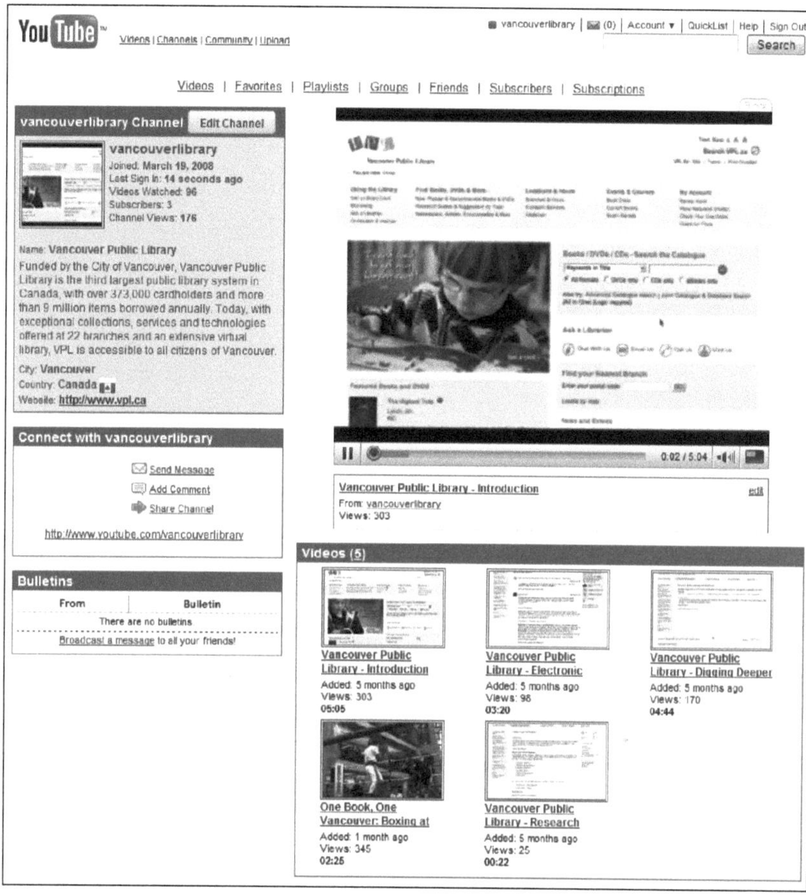

Source: www.youtube.com/user/vancouverlibrary

VPL's Flickr account gives us a space to host photographs promoting the library, and to build connections with the Flickr community (Figure 4.31). Links to Flickr photograph sets are embedded in our events archive on the VPL website, and shared with Flickr groups which focus on VPL. Many of these groups existed before the library joined Flickr, and now we can be involved in their evolution as an active participant rather than a passive bystander.

Figure 4.31 VPL's Flickr photostream – it's not every library that enables you to choose between rock bands and boxing matches when you're looking for events to attend

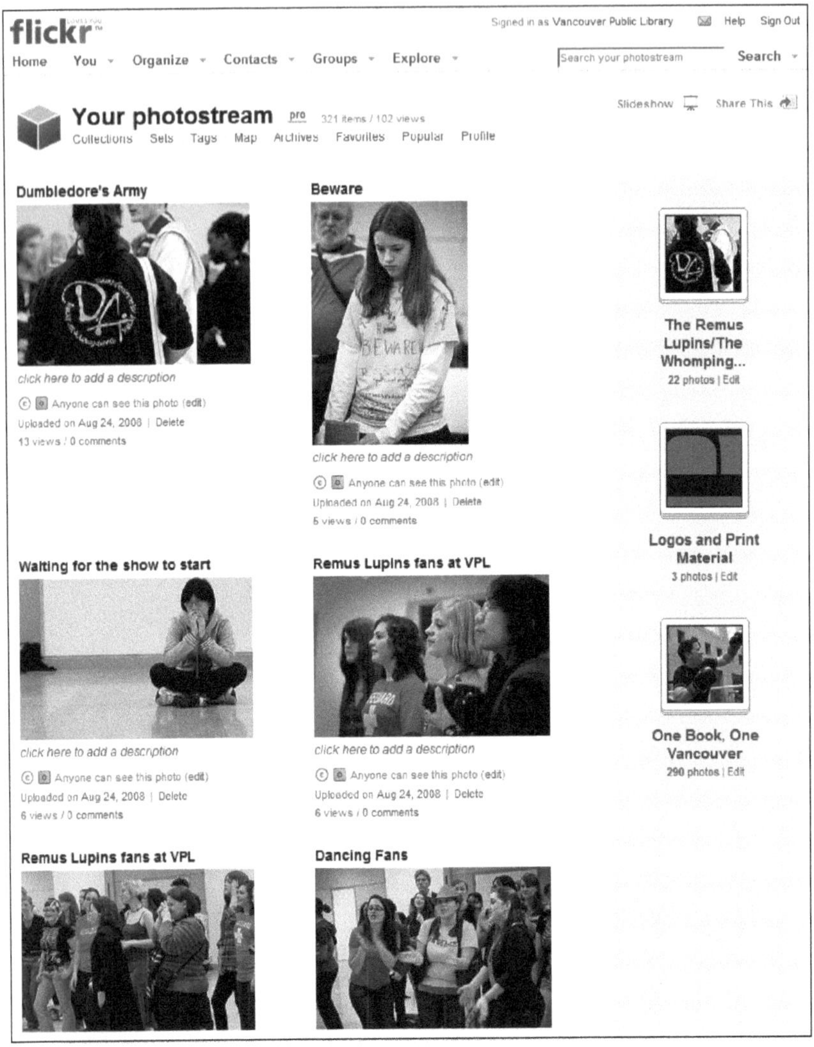

Source: www.flickr.com/photos/vancouverpubliclibrary/

Flickr also provides us with the possibility of carrying out a Library of Congress-style pilot to see if we can enhance the bibliographic data for our own historical photographs collection, and a rich potential source of photographs from the current era.

Events archive

Because both Flickr and YouTube lend themselves so well to event promotion, one of the tools that was built into the library's website was the ability to use the site's content management system to create an events archive that would link to Flickr photographs and YouTube videos on the web. URLs for the relevant photo sets and videos are entered into a template within the CMS, and are then automatically presented as a paired icon and link in the archive entry (Figure 4.32). This allows the library to present the external content while retaining the look and feel of its own website.

Delicious.com

VPL's other foray into Web 2.0 is the use of the social bookmarking site Delicious.com (formerly del.icio.us). Delicious.com allows users to bookmark and tag URLs for easy retrieval and sharing no matter where they are on the web. The library's website includes a collection of more than 5,000 librarian-selected and annotated links. With the redesign and relaunch of the VPL site in February 2008, the library's website redesign team and their development partners, Open Road Communications, opted to move the library's link collection in its entirety to Delicious.com.

Figure 4.32 VPL events archive

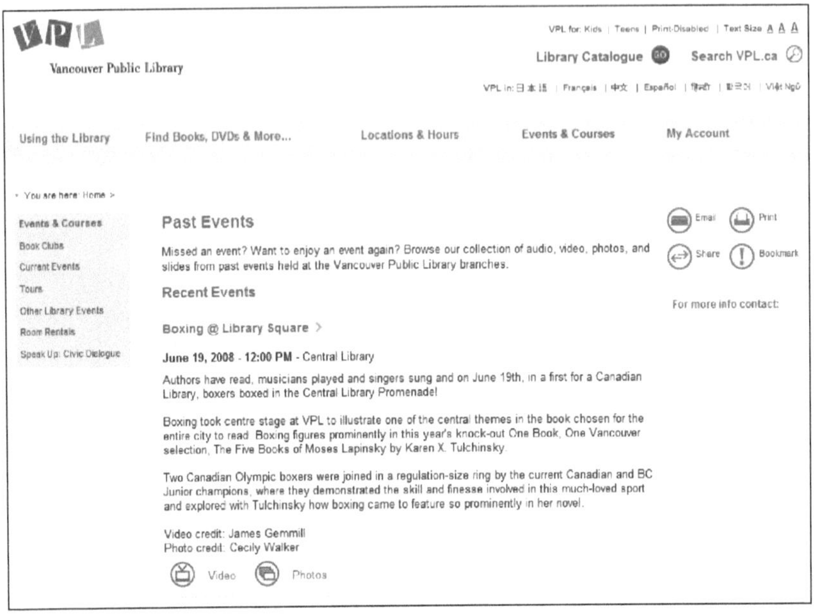

Source: www.vpl.ca/events/archive/

The library's rationale for making such a sweeping change to its link management strategy was threefold. Firstly, an enormous amount of time and effort goes into maintaining the library's link collections. By moving them to Delicious.com, the leading social bookmarking site on the net with more than 3 million registered users and 100 million bookmarked URLs,[4] the library has the potential to reach a far larger audience than it could through the library website alone. This gives us the potential to tap into additional feedback about the value of our link collections, and to track uptake more effectively. (Because links go to external sites, it can be difficult to track their usage with traditional analytics tools.)

Secondly, Delicious.com offers tools – specifically the bookmarklet and Firefox extension – that make creating and annotating a bookmark a matter of a few seconds' work, rather than the laborious HTML coding that was traditionally required to make a link display on the site.

Thirdly, it enabled repurposing of link collections as small sidebars that could be easily inserted on any page of the site using a custom plug-in for the site's Expression Engine content management system. This means that related link lists can be easily placed next to associated content, increasing serendipitous discovery and usability for patrons and boosting use of the links. For example, the 'Computer and Internet' page has a sidebar containing quick links to search engines and e-mail services (www.vpl.ca/library/cat/C410/), and our 'VPL Recommends' page has a sidebar featuring links to literary awards sites (www.vpl.ca/books_dvds_and_more/recommends/).

VPL staff use the Firefox tagging extension to add links to Delicious.com. The library's link collections are arranged by subject, and each collection is given a unique tag – a concatenated string of words which is applied to all links in that collection. So, for example, the internet career search links are given the tag 'busjobnetlinks'. This tag can then be used to generate a Delicious.com URL showing all the career search links: http://feeds.delicious.com/v2/rss/vancouver_public_library/busjobnetlinks (Figure 4.33).

The URL is plugged into a 'Link List' template in the library's content management system, Expression Engine (EE). EE then imports all the links with this tag on to the library's website, where they display as a complete link collection (Figure 4.34).

In addition to the unique tag used to group the links into collections, each link is also given a tag with the name of the subject division responsible for managing that particular link collection, to enable staff to find and edit the links for which they are responsible quickly and easily, and general

Figure 4.33 Career search links on Delicious.com

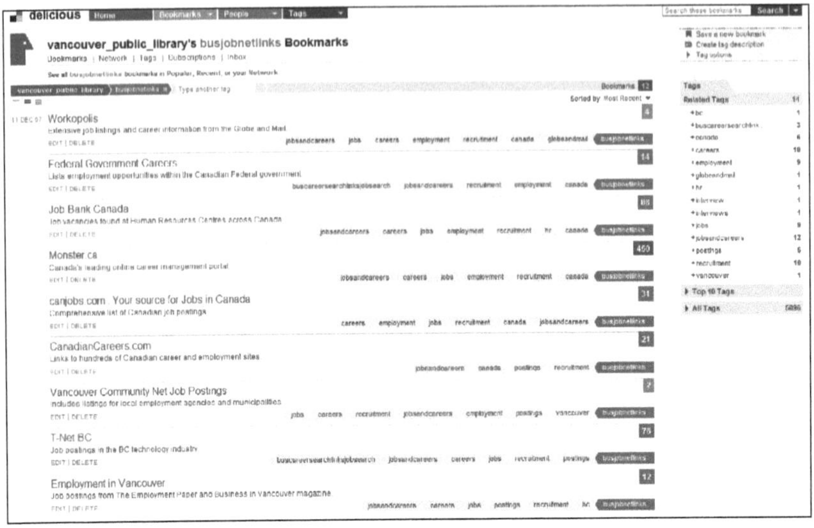

Source: http://delicious.com/vancouver_public_library/busjobnetlinks

Figure 4.34 Career search links on vpl.ca

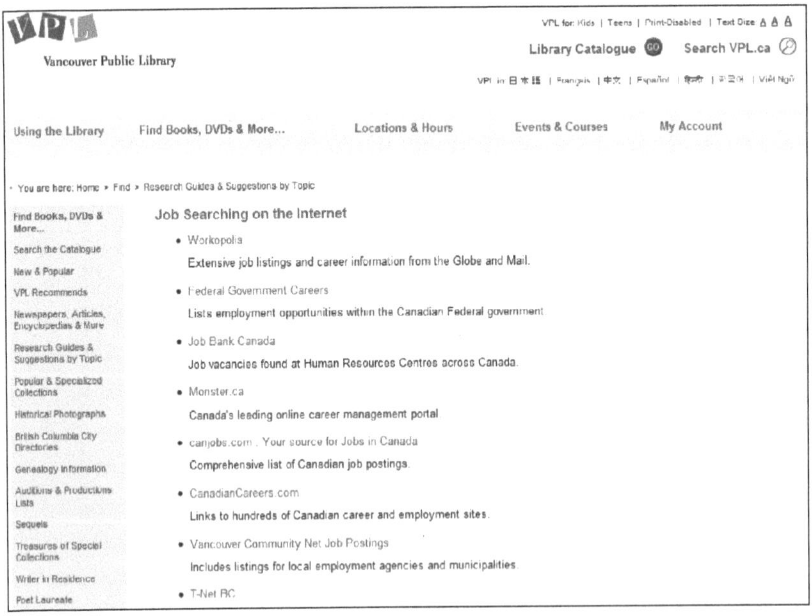

Source: www.vpl.ca/research_guides/related_link_list/4642/

descriptive tags to aid with discovery and sharing on Delicious.com.

VPL's link collections comprise 5,808 unique links and 5,096 individual tags. Almost every link within the collection has an individual annotation provided by librarians, adding value for the casual browser. Moving these collections into Delicious.com means that the entire Delicious.com community will now be able to benefit from the work VPL puts into building, annotating and maintaining these collections, while reducing staff workload within the library.

VPL is also exploring the possibility of working more closely with the Delicious.com community in the future to add greater value to our link collections, in particular investigating Delicious.com tagging conventions to see if our own tagging can be made more meaningful to the community.

Community connections

What we have tried to do with VPL's adoption of Web 2.0 tools and technologies is be extremely strategic about what really adds value to our core web services. In the next chapter, I'll go on to explore some of the main considerations when adding 2.0 functionality to a library's website, and how libraries can ensure that the workload and maintenance of these tools are reasonable.

Notes

1 Raymond, Matt (2008) 'My friend Flickr: a match made in photo heaven', Library of Congress blog, 16 January; available at: *www.loc.gov/blog/?p=233* (accessed: 3 August 2008).

2 Richardson, Gail (2008) 'BiblioCommons emerges: "revolutionary" social discovery system for libraries', *Library Journal*, 19 July; available at: *www.libraryjournal.com/article/CA6579748.html* (accessed: 3 August 2008).
3 Youseffi, Baharak (2008) Personal interview with BiblioCommons liaison librarian, August.
4 Arrington, Michael (2007) 'Exclusive: screenshots and feature overview of the Delicious 2.0 preview', *TechCrunch*, 6 September; available at: *www.techcrunch.com/2007/09/06/exclusive-screen-shots-and-feature-overview-of-delicious-20-preview/* (accessed: 3 August 2008).

5

Controlling the firehose

It's clear that there are huge benefits to welcoming user-generated content into libraries and encouraging communities to engage in conversation and dialogue with their libraries in the virtual space. It's also very apparent that libraries are keen to embrace these new technologies, and have been creative and innovative in using them to promote their services.

However, like any other technology – in fact, like any other significant change to the way we deliver our services – integrating Web 2.0 applications into our websites and managing the content they generate create significant challenges. As we incorporate these new technologies, we need to be aware not just of their potential but also of the likely risks and problems. By flagging these issues in advance, we can build strategies for managing and reducing them.

The technology

Before utilizing new technologies to deliver library services, there are always a couple of nuts-and-bolts questions to answer about the platform.

Integration

The first of these questions is whether a specific platform will integrate with your existing systems. There are such a range of possible tools out there that there's generally something that can fit every platform, not to mention the array of external sites which have no technological dependencies within the library.

Integrating content – from widgets to video – into websites is generally not hard these days; in keeping with the modern web philosophy of making information as portable and reusable as possible, most sites actually do the work for the end user. YouTube provides URLs for every video that enable users to embed that video directly into their own websites; Flickr provides both a URL for individual photographs and a series of widgets that allow users to embed multiple photographs in a variety of layouts.

Integrating technology into the catalogue is harder. Catalogues are legacy applications, notoriously tricky to customize. We're starting to see the first signs of integrating social data into an existing catalogue with projects such as BookSpace and LibraryThing for Libraries. BiblioCommons has shown that it's possible to add a social discovery layer on top of the catalogue in such a way that the user experience is completely seamless. But these are fairly isolated projects, and turning our catalogues into participatory experiences is something that remains beyond the scope of most libraries. Indeed, some libraries are turning to open source solutions to address their need for a more flexible, customizable catalogue, with projects like British Columbia's Evergreen ILS and the Scriblio platform, which is based on WordPress.

Other issues that need to be considered at the integration stage are network security and load. Is the library's bandwidth able to support the increased demand of users actively uploading and downloading content from the site? Are there security implications for the library's network if it offers read/write access to its website?

To minimize the risk of load issues, the library needs to evaluate the new service and its likely uptake. If the service involves a substantial change to the website and existing activity levels, formal load-bearing tests should be carried out in advance to establish whether new hardware and/or increased bandwidth will be required. If this presents a problem, the library may need to turn to external solutions: mashing up rather than building up.

External hosting is also a potential answer to security concerns. If the library would prefer not to run a blog through its own content management system because of the risks of allowing read/write access, a WordPress.com blog can easily be registered and incorporated into the library's site. The blog's content, including all posts and comments, would then be hosted on WordPress servers rather than on the library's own hardware, and additional hosting space can be purchased if required.

Customization

Widgets, gadgets and badges are pretty straightforward. You don't need much in the way of technical expertise to be able to take a small piece of HTML code and paste it into your website. With a more advanced application – say, using the Google Maps API to provide directions to branches – a small amount of programming skill or technical expertise may be required. When it comes to taking something like the Delicious.com API and customizing it to display collections of Delicious.com links on your own website, you need someone with considerable programming knowledge and ability. For larger libraries with substantial systems support in-house, this might not be a huge amount to ask. For smaller libraries, the chances of anyone on staff having this level of programming skill are remote.

The other important question that needs to be addressed when customizing an application is whether or not it can take the load that your library will be asking of it. If it can't, is this something that can be resolved through in-house customization or is it integral to the application? Again, this is not something that will be relevant for every application, but it's an important issue to consider if you're planning to make an application part of your core services – del.icio.us, for example, was experiencing severe slowdowns prior to its relaunch as Delicious.com, to the point where any user who had more than 1,000 collected links found that their collection became virtually unbrowsable. There's no point in offering a link collection, however good, to the del.icio.us community if they're not going to be able to use it because the page load times are so slow.

Support

There's also the question of ongoing technical support. What kind of care and feeding do these applications need? Is it just a case of adding content, or do they require ongoing updates at a technical level? What happens when products are discontinued or updated to a newer version? While it's hard to predict what the future might bring in the way of new applications, one thing that is certain in the current information environment is that nothing that exists right now is going to stay the same for very long. Every application currently in beta is looking at versions 1.0, 2.0, 3.0 and beyond.

Sometimes a new version of an application will have next to no impact for libraries. They may not even realize that there's a newer, shinier version of the widget they embedded six months ago available. However, the deeper an application is integrated into the library's systems, the more significant the effect is likely to be. To cite a recent example from personal experience, at the end of July 2008 the site then known as del.icio.us renamed itself Delicious.com, changing its URL and replacing its API in the process. While rumours and promises of del.icio.us 2.0 had been circulating on the web for some time previously, there was no indication of how radical the changes to the API would be – nor that the original API would immediately be removed with no time for testing or migration. Every one of Vancouver Public Library's external web links broke when the change was made, and it took a frantic eight hours of the developer's time to restore them. Web editors within the library then had to go through every link list, updating the Delicious.com URL to reflect the changes.

In an ideal world there would have been notice of the change, and Delicious.com would have continued offering the original API in parallel with the new version for long enough to give developers a chance to make any changes required before switching over. But the fact is that Delicious.com makes its API available for free, for other people to benefit from, and it has no obligation to the developers who use it. It's one of the dangers of mashing up rather than building up: if you become reliant on an external service, you're also dependent on the direction that it decides is appropriate for its platform. And it's one thing for a crisis like this to happen in a large library system with immediate access to the programming skill required to fix it; it would be quite another for a library that had paid to have a system like this developed, but had no in-house personnel or external contractors on hand to apply an immediate fix when the problem occurred.

Sustainability

The other challenge with using external tools to enhance web services is that in addition to unexpected (or even expected) changes, decisions about the long-term viability of the tool are in someone else's hands. The risks do vary depending on who created the tool and how stable the company or community behind it is, but ultimately you're dealing with someone else's product – and because so many of them are available for free, there's no technical support contract or obligation for them to keep supplying the service the way there would be with a purchased product.

With open source tools, those that have been around for a while generally have a strong community behind them. User tech forums are a rich source of information and expertise if something goes wrong, or isn't working the way you expected. This gives libraries somewhere to turn in the case of technical difficulties or failure. In fact, the library may even resolve some of the problems internally, share its solution and subsequently become a valued contributor to that community. However, newer open source tools may have been created *ad hoc*, or without any plan for permanence or development. It's worth being cautious with new or beta tools, and not becoming too reliant on them until they've shown some longevity and evidence of community support.

Products developed by private companies are also worth treating with caution. How long has the company been around? How much has it invested in this particular product? Is there evidence of an ongoing plan for development and support? If the product itself is free, where are the company's revenues coming from? A significant risk is that many companies will offer a product for free while it's in early-stage or beta testing, and then require payment or subscription at a later stage. If you're using a tool that's in beta or recently released and there's no obvious commitment to keep it free of charge, consider whether it's something you'd be prepared to pay for in the future or whether there are alternative free tools which can provide a similar service.

Extending your library's web presence on to external websites is another area where you're placing yourselves firmly in the hands of a third party. What happens if it changes the format of the site, or the company goes under or is bought out and the site ceases to exist? If you've simply placed a static page there, it probably won't affect you much, but there's also very little benefit in having a page that doesn't evolve, change or make any effort to engage users. The more time and effort you invest in creating content that exists outside of a library's web space, the higher the risk if the host for that content suffers any kind of problem.

One of the best ways to mitigate this is to use these channels for topical, current content: for example, using Twitter primarily to highlight library events. If anything happens to the platform then the channel is lost, but you won't lose original content that you've invested a significant amount of time in creating. Of course, this technique works better on some platforms than others (a WordPress blog containing teen reviews, for example, is entirely composed of original content), but it's one step you can take to minimize the risk of keeping library content on external websites. Another should go without saying: if you do create original content on an external site, ensure that you always have back-up copies stored on your own server.

Any time you choose to work with external products and applications without a formal contract or agreement of any kind, there is a risk that the product will change radically or even be pulled from the market without warning. Part of developing organizational policies and plans around the use of Web 2.0 tools and technologies (a subject that will be addressed in more detail later in this chapter) is ensuring that you have a back-up strategy in place should the technology be removed from the market, suddenly incur an unanticipated cost or change so radically that it no longer fits the purpose for which you intended to use it.

Mash up versus build up

In terms of both integration and sustainability, libraries investigating the use of Web 2.0 technologies need to ask themselves exactly which applications are appropriate for the level of technical support and expertise they can provide. One of the great things about Web 2.0 technologies is that they're completely scalable. There's something out there that can enhance every library website, regardless of the size of the library or the amount of technical support it can offer.

This is where the mash-up versus build-up philosophy becomes increasingly important. By building a new tool from scratch, or heavily customizing an existing tool, it's certainly possible to achieve more seamless integration and a smoother end-user experience. But this requires time, dedication and programming expertise, not to mention the kind of ongoing technical support and maintenance discussed above, and isn't always necessary to bring added value to the users.

It's an important question for libraries to ask: do you need to build your own blog when you can easily integrate a

WordPress blog into your existing site – and even access it under your own domain name for just $10 per year? Do you need to build your own RSS feeds for new titles when you could use a LibraryThing widget to display them on the front page of the site? Do you need to set up your own video hosting when you can just as easily host videos on YouTube, where there's an established community, commenting functionality and the ability to embed the video player in your own site to share content?

In an ideal world we would all be able to create exactly the tools we needed, whenever we needed them. But one of the great things about Web 2.0 is that it espouses a philosophy of sharing and pooling expertise to create tools that are easily repurposed for different scenarios. There's no point reinventing the wheel unless you need to; in spite of the questions around ongoing support and sustainability, plus the inherent risk in using a third-party application to deliver services, these are often outweighed by the ease of taking an existing tool and integrating it into your site. With the multitude of tools available on the web, even if a company or entrepreneur discontinues the application that you've been using, chances are you'll be able to find another one that performs a similar function. And the time it takes to switch one application for another is almost certainly going to be less than the lost development time if a customized application ceases to be offered, or requires extensive work due to API changes.

Choosing wisely

We're working right now in a very rich environment. It seems that every week, if not every day, we're seeing a flood of new products and tools hit the market. When it comes to selecting the best tools to include on library websites, there's almost an embarrassment of riches to choose from. This makes one of the biggest challenges knowing exactly which tools to select, or which external websites to use to engage with users. It's really hard to know if today's big thing will last: by tomorrow it may have been swallowed up by a bigger company, superseded by a newer version or eclipsed by something faster and shinier. The moment you log on to the web and start searching for widgets, APIs, applications and tools, the bandwagons start rolling past in such numbers that it's tempting just to grab the nearest one and climb on.

Avoiding fads

Avoiding fads is challenging. As discussed in the first chapter, it's really important that we respond to the trends emerging on the internet. We need to do so to remain relevant to our users. But this doesn't mean we should neglect to take the time for thoughtful evaluation of new technologies and web services to ensure they really are bringing value to our patrons. What this requires is a careful balance between evaluation and responsiveness: having a framework in place to ensure that we understand both the risks inherent in a particular tool or technology and the potential value it brings to library services and users.

The first step is to ensure that selected technologies really do offer added value to library patrons. So what's the best way to go about this? Traditionally, this kind of information has been gathered using methods such as surveys and focus groups. There's no better method of finding out what our users want than going out and asking them. However, it's important that any traditional survey method reaches current non-users as well as users of the library. If we can find out what services would have enough appeal to non-users to bring them into the library, we can build services specifically targeted towards those people and help them understand what the library may be able to offer them.

Another rich and potentially very useful source of information is the collected community dialogue on the internet. There are two kinds of very valuable information that can be captured in this dialogue: conversation about your library, highlighting areas where there's audience interest in library services and engagement should be easier; and views from other libraries, whether it's their opinion on the latest tools or neat applications that they've found for a new technology.

Capturing the useful parts of this aggregated community dialogue requires a combination of observing general trends and going out and searching for specific information. For example, we're all aware of the enormous popularity of the Amazon interface, which offers not just opportunities for reviewing and rating but discovery tools that make recommendations based on people who purchased similar items. Tools such as Shelfari and LibraryThing, which enable internet users to create an online library and review, rate and share items they own or have read, have seen a huge surge in popularity over the past couple of years. These wider trends are easily observed and offer useful information to anyone looking for ways to increase interest and engagement in books and reading.

Searching can be a little more challenging. There are some site-specific or vertical search engines that make it relatively simple to take a particular website and find out if your library has been a topic of conversation there. Twitter Search, for example, allows you to search all public tweets posted on Twitter, and in the case study in the last chapter

Vancouver Public Library was able to take advantage of this and establish that VPL services and programs were something that featured quite regularly in the conversation of Vancouver area Twitter members. From this VPL staff learned that Twitter had an audience with a proven interest in library services: a natural target for engagement with a library Twitter feed. The enthusiastic response of the users who have signed up to the VPL feed is a clear endorsement of this being a service that adds value by delivering library news and events updates directly to them, rather than them having to seek this information out on the library's site.

Google's site-specific search can be a great way of searching individual sites for public content about your library. Using the command site:[URL] before your keywords in the Google search box limits your results to content from that site (Figure 5.1), which is a huge help when searching a social networking site for content relating to an organization.

It's often amazing what you can learn from carrying out these kinds of searches. From the test search illustrated in Figure 5.1, I learned that flash mobbers are using Facebook to organize a 'silent rave' event (ten minutes of dancing to music heard only through headphones) outside Vancouver's Central Library a few days from now. Something to watch out for!

Likewise, a quick site search on Flickr or YouTube can be a great way of finding out what kind of interest there is in your library, and where that interest is focused. A Flickr group about your building's architecture might give you entirely different ideas than a Facebook group formed around a particular library event.

RSS aggregators like Bloglines, Google Reader and Netvibes can be another good way to monitor for both conversation and information. These aggregators allow you

Figure 5.1 Sample Google search, limited by site to Facebook

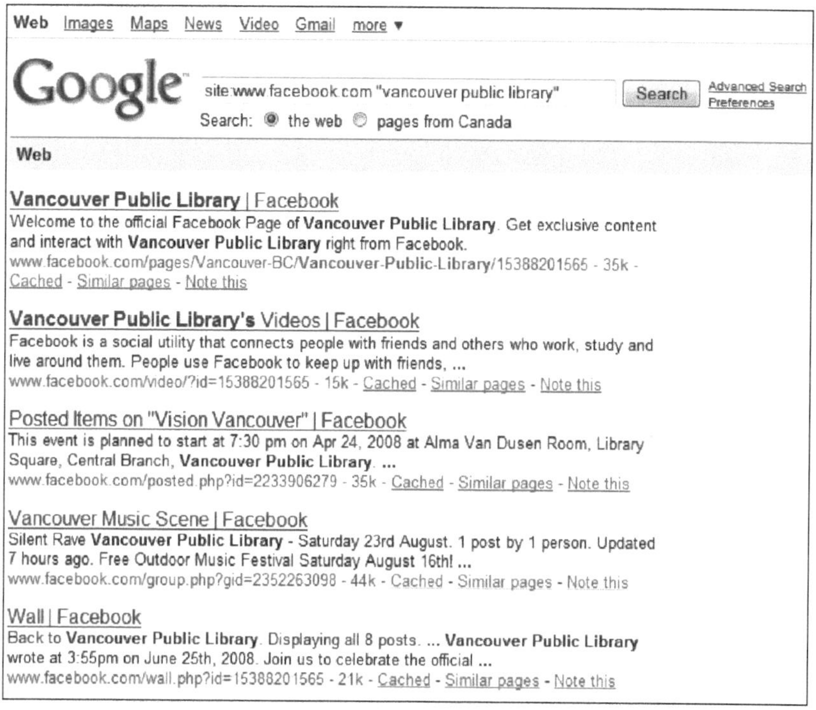

to subscribe to your favourite blogs or websites, and notify you when new posts or content are added. Monitoring the blogosphere, in particular, can be a rich source of additional information about what other libraries are doing with the latest tools and technologies. Librarians are a creative, collaborative bunch, and there are many great blogs out there written either by the innovators themselves or by people who are observing and commenting on those innovations. We're lucky enough to be a part of a profession that is all about the 2.0 spirit: library services in different provinces, states or countries don't have to worry about competing with each other, because we all have separate user bases and the same ultimate goal of increasing literacy, learning and love of books, reading and information. It's second nature for us to share our great ideas with each other. For a library looking to introduce new services, having a model that has proven successful for other libraries on which to base those services definitely helps mitigate the risk that it won't be worthwhile for users, or that it will turn out to be just a passing fad.

In terms of assessing which sites are worthwhile venues for libraries to establish an external presence, the first thing to look at is whether there is any kind of local presence or network which indicates that people from within the library's geographic catchment area are using the site. For larger sites, this might be a relatively small percentage of the overall user base. The important thing is that there's evidence that people from the library's municipality or district are using the site, and that it can be used to connect with them. It's not all about the Facebooks and MySpaces, although the size and popularity of these sites are more or less a guarantee that libraries will find users from their demographic area spending time there. Local community sites might also be a great venue for library partnerships.

Once this has been established, user base and activity levels are the key factors in determining whether the site is likely to be a viable long-term host for library content. How many registered users does the site have, and what kind of activity is it generating? How active are the particular demographic that the library is interested in? (You're not building a Facebook page in order to engage with all 100 million of its registered users.) If they're inactive, is it possible that library content can pique their interest and encourage them to engage?

While you do want to avoid fads, it's important to remain open and willing to trying new things. If you're really unsure about whether a new web product is going to last or appeal to users, evaluate the amount of time it will take to implement and whether this is worth the risk. Then if you go ahead, treat it as a pilot project that you can reassess at intervals.

If you build it, will they come?

Simply adding a blog or wiki to your website, or creating a MySpace profile or Facebook page, is absolutely no guarantee that your users will visit those pages or post content to your blog. You need to have a clear strategy in mind for generating interest and encouraging participation.

First of all, have a marketing strategy for your new service. To introduce the service to existing users, promote it on the homepage of the library's website, or through your news feed if you have one. It's also worth creating leaflets or flyers that you can hand to users when they're checking out books, or leave by your library's internet workstations. Posters in strategic spots can also be an effective way of spreading awareness. Take advantage of all the typical publicity strategies that you would use to promote any new library service.

If your library runs classes or training courses that focus on web products, consider holding one targeted at the type of technology you're using. Library patrons who have never posted to a wiki or blog before may not be sure how the tools work, and having a library instructor teach them the skills they need might give them enough confidence to get involved – not to mention being a good way of promoting the new service.

Use any feeds that you have to tell people about the service. If you're already running a Twitter feed that provides library updates, or you have a news feed on your library website, these can be great venues for promotion. Many websites also have built-in marketing features for organizations; for example, Facebook pages allow you to send an update to all Facebook users who have registered as fans of that page.

Target specific groups within the library who are already engaged to get the ball rolling. For example, if you're starting an online book club introduce it at the library's existing book clubs. Demonstrate how to post to a discussion to help build confidence, and showcase successful existing online book clubs to show people how the discussion can evolve. If you're relying on a specific group of library users to generate content – say, for example, a blog containing teen book reviews – provide them with support and encouragement. Consider holding book review meetings at the library; attendees could choose books to read and learn how to post reviews.

Make sure that the tool is pre-seeded with content to catch people's interest. Interested library staff can post initial book reviews, or kick-start the discussions on a new book. If you're looking at something like a Facebook or MySpace page, ensure that it is updated with new content regularly to encourage people both to keep coming back and to participate themselves.

It's worth keeping in mind that although it's important to choose your tools carefully, a lot of the items discussed in this book require a minimal time investment to get up and running. Twitter updates literally take a matter of a moment or two to post, and adding a discussion to a Facebook page to encourage people to talk about favorite books or library events is equally quick and easy. If you're not sure which web tools and sites are the best ones to engage your users, start small and treat each one as an individual pilot. See if the interest and uptake are there, and if not do some basic analysis: has the tool been promoted sufficiently? Or has it had plenty of exposure, but failed to generate interest regardless?

If they come, can they get in?

One of the most important decisions you will be making for your new service is that if it includes the option for patron contributions, how they will authenticate and/or register themselves? We know from long experience that authentication can be a serious barrier to access for patrons, particularly when separate logins are required for different areas of the library site. Patron frustrations include having to remember their card number, or actually have their card to hand; remembering their PIN; and having to log in separately for access to catalogue functions and other electronic resources.

Unfortunately, registration is also a protective measure that helps provide accountability and reduces the risk of some of the problems associated with online discussions, such as flamewars and trolling. Being able to link specific users to their library accounts enables the library to follow through on significant incidents. This all contributes to a pleasant atmosphere and a reduction in the workload around moderation. Some form of registration is also required to enable users to maintain a history and, if desired, a recognizable individual presence on the site.

Keeping in mind that the majority of library websites already require at least two separate logins ('My Account' functionality; subscription databases), the most important thing about adding in a third is to keep it simple. Ideally all that should be required for regular login is a user name and password, both selected by the patron. If the library wants the user's library card number for accountability purposes, it should be recorded at the initial registration stage but not required for future logins. Ideally the library won't require a library card number to participate in the conversation, as this automatically excludes any library user (or non-user) who doesn't have a card.

The users' public profiles should always be under their control to address privacy concerns, with the option to make any or all content private.

Workload

One of the hardest things about embracing new technologies – especially moving to embrace them quickly and responsively – is the issue of workload. Every time you take on a new project, it means considering the impact on staff workload and the organization as a whole. Incorporating user-generated content on your website and engaging users in other web spaces can be a source of considerable extra work for staff, and managing this effectively is challenging.

Creating content

The level of work involved in content creation on the library's part is a critical issue when launching a new web-based service or expanding the library's web presence to an external site. As mentioned previously, seeding new tools and services like wikis and blogs with content so that users can see how they work and become interested in participating is vital. The question then becomes how much effort is required to maintain it on an ongoing basis? Much of this depends on the nature of the tool you choose and the kind of content it is intended to host.

A book review blog, once established, may well become self-propagating. The more interest and involvement there is, the more users will generate their own content. The librarians may need to step in occasionally to suggest new titles to review or provide information in a comments thread, but their job is to review and moderate the user-generated content rather than actively contributing content themselves. (Unless they choose to, of course – in practice it's quite hard to keep a librarian out of a discussion about books!)

A MySpace or Facebook page is likely to need more in the way of ongoing content creation. Users will expect to see new content appearing on the library's Facebook page, otherwise there's little to draw them back to the page and encourage them to participate in discussions and wall posts. Posting updates about library events is quick, easy, keeps the page current and doubles up as a promotional tool. Posting fresh discussions when previous ones turn stale is also a good idea; you don't want to swamp the page with discussion topics, but you want actively to encourage people to engage with each other and with the library. Introduce new services on the page, and encourage users to share their opinions.

The actual effort of ongoing content creation isn't likely to be a huge workload issue; moderation and review are far more significant. What is really important is that updates happen on a regular basis to keep content current and give users a reason to keep checking back. This means assigning specific responsibility for updating content to one or more librarians, and ensuring that this becomes a regular part of their work routine.

If they come, will they behave?

This is one of the most time-consuming and treacherous areas of managing user-generated content. The purpose of introducing these kinds of tools and services is to encourage users to participate, to engage in active dialogue with the library. But this also means that the content they create is captured as part of the library's community archive. The role of moderator – especially for a public institution that is funded by the taxpayer and typically associated with intellectual freedom and the fight against censorship – is not one that comes easily to many libraries.

As a precautionary measure, before you launch any of these tools on your website make sure that you have both a clear disclaimer absolving the library from responsibility for the content that is posted and a 'terms of service' agreement that users must read and sign up to when they register. It's actually surprising how few libraries lay out clear terms of service or policy guidelines for users who are contributing web content. The terms of service should include expected rules of behavior (netiquette) for the site, and clear descriptions of the kind of content that is not tolerated. A thorough terms of service agreement will generally cover:

- legal disclaimer (this absolves the library of any responsibility for content, and also gives it the right to review and remove content as it considers appropriate);
- copyright (guidelines around expectations for citing sources and not infringing copyright);
- advertising (commercial use of the service or use for advertising a for-profit business is normally barred);
- privacy (if your library has an existing privacy policy in place, you may choose to treat all personal data gathered

as part of the web service according to that policy; otherwise this will need to be laid out clearly);

- ownership of content (the library may choose to assume ownership of all content posted to its site, or leave ownership in the hands of the authors);
- illegal material (posting is barred – you may want to give examples of the kinds of material that would be covered under this, e.g. libel, slander, etc.);
- abuse (netiquette expectations and consequences of abuse).

Many terms of service are extremely lengthy and full of legal jargon, so it's also a good idea to have a very simple and clear set of instructions for users as well: 'Basically we're asking you to be respectful of others and not post anything offensive, abusive or illegal.'

Of all these items, abuse is generally the hardest one to define and to moderate. Wherever you get large groups of people interacting – either online or offline – disagreements will inevitably happen, and there is a risk that at some point the conversation will degenerate into a flamewar. The relative anonymity of online forums often encourages people to speak out more aggressively than they would if they were talking face to face with someone, and many internet forums are plagued with trolls – users whose sole purpose is to post controversial, off-topic or insulting messages with the intention of stirring up trouble. This can be mitigated by having a registration process that includes the user's library card number or e-mail address so that there is a degree of accountability built in, but this also acts as a barrier to access to anyone without a library card. Part of the purpose of opening up our websites for user participation is to engage individuals who currently do not use the library, making this somewhat counterproductive.

Be very clear in your terms of service about what constitutes abuse. It's not necessarily just personal insults; abuse can also include posting other people's personal information online, deliberately making offensive posts targeted at certain individuals, deliberate posting of off-topic content, creating alias accounts to harass certain users or push particular points of view, and persistent downrating (where a user rating system is in place) of targeted users. It's also a good idea to emphasize abuse policies by focusing on what it's not: encouraging users to treat each other's opinions with respect.

This is where it can be a good idea to introduce an FAQ or help section that explains things in clearer language than the terms of service. Users are more likely to access an FAQ regularly; realistically, most will probably never look at the terms of service again after they register. An FAQ can also be a really good venue to address known problems that have arisen on the forum, blog or wiki.

Here is an example of netiquette guidance:

> Remember that online, as in any discussion, not everyone is going to agree with each other all the time. Be prepared for a free exchange of opinions and views. When you disagree with an opinion, try to keep focused on explaining what you think is wrong about that opinion, and why, rather than what you think is wrong with the person expressing it. Above all, be respectful. It's far more effective winning people over to your point of view with logic than battering them into submission with insults.

Or, as LibraryThing puts it: 'Be nice, please.'[1]

Moderating content, particularly where interpersonal disagreements occur, can often mean walking a fine line. It's best to keep moderation as impersonal as possible, based purely on breaches of the terms of service. If people associate moderation with a particular librarian or personal account, it becomes too easy to throw around accusations of bias or favoritism when a post is deleted or a user account banned. Posts should be reviewed regularly and posts that breach the site policies removed promptly, with a formal e-mail advising the poster of the reason for removal.

Another very tricky area to moderate is 'off-topic' comment. If your terms of service are clear, it's relatively easy to flag most abusive and/or offensive posts: the risk is more in the user response than the deletion of the post. Off-topic is harder. You might have a very open forum where general discussion is encouraged; in this case, there's probably very little that you would consider off-topic. This can be beneficial in terms of both encouraging dialogue and helping users feel comfortable in the environment. But you might also have a very specific forum where you want to keep dialogue focused on the topic at hand: say, a virtual book club where you don't want the discussion to stray too far from the current book of the month.

A good middle ground when considering whether to remove content for being off-topic is whether it has evolved naturally from the original discussion. For example, a user might have read a book on vacation, and while talking about the book they end up digressing to their experiences on that vacation. This is clearly harmless and not an intentional attempt to hijack the course of the discussion, and removing it will only lead to bad feeling among users. It's far better to intervene as the discussion leader, much as you would if leading an offline book club, and guide the discussion gently back towards the book. On the other hand, if someone jumps into a conversation about themes in a family saga and starts trying to divert the conversation to politics or the value of hosting the Olympic Games, this is a deliberately off-topic post that should be removed.

Some communities try to deal with these kinds of off-topic posts by providing a general discussion area, or even a single open thread, where people are free to talk about anything they like. This is generally an effective way of keeping the main discussions on topic, but bear in mind that you will need to apply the same moderation standards to this content when it comes to abuse, illegal content, advertising and any other items from the terms of service. This will require a further time investment, but these kinds of open forums can be a great source of user opinion and views.

One option which is growing in popularity among online discussion forums is to introduce mechanisms to allow the community to be, as far as possible, self-moderating. In self-moderating forums, posts (blog comments, book reviews, etc.) have a 'Report This' or 'Flag Abuse' button. If users come across a post which they consider to be abusive, offensive or otherwise in breach of the rules, they click the button. If a certain number of individual users – say three, for example – all report the same post, the post is then suspended and reviewed by a moderator. If the moderator finds the post is not in breach of the rules it can be reinstated, but if it does breach the rules it will be permanently deleted and a warning sent to the poster. Some sites will follow up by permanently banning users who have more than a certain number of posts removed for abuse.

This self-moderating system is used by BiblioCommons, with the added feature that users can choose to ignore one another. Every user profile has 'Trust' and 'Ignore' buttons built in. 'Trust' allows users to flag people with a similar taste in books so that they can follow their posts; clicking 'Ignore' means they will not be able to see anything that particular user posts anywhere on the site. When disputes occur between users that are simply differences of opinion rather than breaching the terms of service, BiblioCommons staff encourage use of the 'Ignore' button to prevent the dispute from recurring or becoming more heated. This leaves the responsibility for appropriate behavior very much in the hands of the individual users, as they have full control over whether or not they can see posts made by users with dissenting opinions from their own.

Where possible, self-moderation is very much the preferred route for dealing with problem content. It gives the community control over what they perceive to be offensive, and puts the onus on them to flag inappropriate content promptly. It also lessens the workload for the official moderators, as they only need to step in and review content when it has been flagged by enough users. However, not all software tools provide self-moderation options, so implementing it may require additional back-end work by library systems staff.

At the opposite extreme is the model used by many bloggers, which is to queue all submitted comments and have them reviewed by a moderator before they are posted to the blog. While this puts complete control of all published content in the hands of the library and ensures that an inappropriate comment will never be missed during a content review, it also largely defeats the purpose of trying to have a true dialogue with users. The asynchronous nature of these kinds of posts, where comments show up en masse and often hours after they were originally posted, discourages open, conversational online discourse. It's pretty much the same as the difference between addressing an e-mail reference question and answering a reference question using live chat, where you can go back and forth with the user and ask as many follow-up questions as you need.

This kind of moderation increases the workload for the library exponentially, as every comment needs to be individually reviewed. The review process would have to be built into an individual librarian's workload as at least a daily task – preferably several times a day, as the longer the delay the more fractured the attempted dialogue becomes – and the library would also be officially approving every published comment, which could cause problems if a comment were published which led to user complaints. This very controlled moderation could be used effectively on a platform where content is more static – for example, screening book reviews before posting would not significantly impact on the quality of the dialogue – but is not likely to be as viable an option on any platform where a back-and-forth dialogue between the library and its users, or between the users themselves, is expected.

Moderation of user-generated content is essential, which is why it's so important to build into the terms of service that the library has the right to edit, remove or reuse content as it deems appropriate. Clear site policies to which every user agrees on sign-up give the library an essential veto power over content posted to its website.

Moderation is also hard. Deleting posts is sometimes a no-brainer, but inevitably sooner or later it's going to lead to an upset user who disagrees with the reason for removal and feels that they have been unfairly censored. This is where it can be particularly hard for a library, normally the champion of intellectual freedom, to act as a moderator. A good parallel to draw is that the same behavioral standards apply on a library-run discussion forum as in the library itself. If someone stood in the middle of the library shouting and swearing at other patrons, it's unlikely that library staff would just stand by and let it happen. It's the same online. We need to make our online forums a welcoming but safe environment where users feel comfortable interacting and sharing thoughts, ideas and opinions.

From a workload perspective, you need to give careful thought to how your chosen moderation method will fit into staff's day-to-day routines. If you opt to allow the community to be predominantly self-moderating, more work will be required developing the system and establishing workflows but the actual moderation process will be less time-consuming, as library staff will only need to step in when a post has been flagged by a certain number of people and temporarily suspended. At the other end of the spectrum, screening all posts requires considerably more time on the part of the moderator, and will also need to be regularly scheduled at frequent intervals to ensure that comments don't become too disjointed. The middle (and most common) ground is to allow free posting but to review posts regularly and encourage users to notify staff if they see an abusive or offensive post. This combination still requires regular review on the part of staff, and this should be built into day-to-day workflows to ensure that it does not get neglected or forgotten.

Moderation is also an area where it's easy to become the victim of your own success. The more active and popular your community, the more time it will take to review posts and the greater the likelihood of problems occurring. This is one of the risks of opening up your website to dialogue. But by establishing clear guidelines at the outset, and encouraging the kind of welcoming, supportive atmosphere where people feel comfortable and confident both in posting themselves and in flagging problem posts for attention, you can help ensure that the community develop along these lines. If you establish a strong community with a solid user base it's often surprising how much ownership they take over the community space, and how quick the community will be to address problems in their midst if and when they occur. Striking the right balance between easy, barrier-free access and accountability can be tough, but if you have a committed community they will often prove to be your biggest aid in effectively moderating and managing the resulting conversation.

Organization

So you've built your platform and chosen your tools, and people have come. You're accumulating quite a stack of book reviews, ratings, comments and discussion threads. Your website has become a conversation rather than a lecture, and you're learning all kinds of interesting things about your users and how they perceive and interact with the library. The question is, what do you do with that content now? Do you keep it, discard it after a certain length of time, or overlay some system of organization to allow users to browse through the collected dialogue of the community?

Much user-generated content is completely informal: for example, the ebb and flow of conversation on a discussion forum thread. But depending on how far you're willing to go in opening up your content for user input, other content is more formal and requires a more formal system of classification. For example, if your library produces study guides and has typically included those guides in the catalogue, what happens when you turn those guides into wikis and allow community experts to contribute?

In terms of organizing and finding information, the key with user-generated content is discovery rather than formal classification. The whole ethos of Web 2.0 has evolved around the effectiveness of keywords, natural language and bottom-up folksonomical organization rather than formal hierarchies and classification schemata. By incorporating the ability for users to tag content – for example, individual books or blog posts – you enable users to build a classification system using the kind of terminology and labels that make sense to them. By making the aggregated tags available to other users, you're creating a system of serendipitous discovery where users can browse tags to find content related to topics they're interested in.

These informal folksonomies don't represent the kind of highly controlled, hierarchical classification we were taught in library school, but they represent an enormous enhancement of the user experience. There's also no reason why folksonomies can't exist alongside the more formal classification systems: LibraryThing, for example, offers user tags as part of the catalogue record for an individual item, and BiblioCommons provides related tags as a browsing option along with related subject headings drawn directly from the catalogue. More and more we're seeing a crossover of traditional classification systems with these kinds of informal, user-created folksonomies; as librarians, our obligation is not to choose the system that makes the most sense for us and force our users to learn it (which has tended to be our approach in the past) but to make sure our users have access to the system that makes the most sense for them, and enhance that where we can with our own knowledge and understanding.

Introducing tagging of content usually requires some customization on the library's part, although it is possible to purchase third-party data or applications such as LibraryThing and BiblioCommons. Many content management systems incorporate tagging modules, so libraries running database-driven websites may have relatively easy access to tagging functionality. Most blogging software also includes tagging of individual posts as standard, although this has to be done by the post creator rather than users who are reading and commenting, which does limit the scope somewhat.

Goals and success measures

Part of ensuring that your new tools and applications are bringing value is having a very clear set of goals and success measures laid out from the start. Some of these goals may be purely qualitative; but if you can also incorporate some hard quantitative targets it will make it considerably easier to evaluate whether or not you have achieved success.

Some sample goals could be:

- to engage library users in dialogue;
- to incorporate user-generated content on the library website;
- to reach non-users of the library and introduce them to library services, programs and events.

Sample success measures or key performance indicators for a blog could include:

- *xx* user blog posts per month;
- *xx* user comments per month;
- increase in posting activity of at least *x* per cent over the first six months;
- increase in commenting activity of at least *xx* per cent over the first six months;
- *xxx* hits on the blog per month.

Sample success measures or KPIs for a wiki may include:

- *xx* users contributing per month;
- *xx* entries modified per user per month;
- *xxx* hits on the wiki homepage per month;
- *xxx* hits on individual wiki pages per month.

Sample success measures or KPIs for a discussion forum could be:

- *xx* new users registered per month;
- *xx* new discussions posted per month;
- at least *xx* responses posted per discussion thread;
- *xxx* total responses posted per month;
- *xxx* hits on the forum per month.

Sample success measures or KPIs for a Facebook page might include:

- *xx* new fans per month;
- *xx* wall posts by users per month;
- *xx* new discussions per month;
- *xx* discussion responses per month;
- *xxx* unique page views per month (trackable using Facebook's statistics package).

Other potential success measures that could be applied to any user-generated content platform include:

- *xx* per cent increase in registered users per month;
- *xx* per cent increase in overall participation per month;
- *xx* per cent increase in overall posting activity per month;
- *xx* per cent increase in overall hits/page views per month.

If you hand out feedback or evaluation forms at the end of library programs or events, it's possible to obtain figures for the number of users who heard about those activities via the library's Twitter feed or Facebook page.

It's also useful to keep an eye on your overall website statistics whenever you launch a new web service or application, particularly one whose purpose is to engage users and encourage them to interact with the library. If you see a jump or a slow, steady increase in overall use of your website, or a shift in the balance between use of the website and use of the catalogue, this can be evidence of new services creating an incentive to visit and driving traffic to the library's site.

Organizational buy-in

For new services to succeed, it's completely essential to make sure they have organizational support and buy-in. This ensures that the staff time required for development and maintenance of the service will be made available, and that staff are willing to participate in promoting and using the new service.

With user-generated content, this can be a challenge. As discussed earlier in this book, opening ourselves up in this way requires a sea change in the way we think of ourselves and our services. It means accepting a position as facilitators rather than experts, guides rather than instructors; it means discarding some of our traditional notions of authority and acknowledging the value that exists in conversation, dialogue and community expertise. It means taking a different view of our role as the curator of community knowledge and experience. It also means adopting new tools and technologies, which requires the development of new skill sets in order to use these tools and technologies effectively. While some librarians are hugely enthused about the possibilities that Web 2.0 and online user engagement offer, others see them as something distinctly separate from the traditional core library services and may be harder to convince.

Building the case for the value of new web services is absolutely key for ensuring staff support. Although it's easy enough to pilot new services, make sure that you're clearly able to demonstrate why they're worth piloting. You should have clear measures of success laid out in advance, and a plan for moving pilot services into day-to-day operations if they do succeed.

A good way of encouraging staff buy-in is to organize demonstrations or training sessions where you can showcase other libraries that have successfully incorporated these kinds of tools and the content they generate, and use these examples to illustrate how those libraries have benefited.

Similarly, if you know staff are concerned about the technical skills required to use and run web-based services, hold training sessions to introduce the tools to staff and help build their skill sets and knowledge. A training session on adding collections to LibraryThing, bookmarking using Delicious.com or learning to use a blog or wiki can be a lot of fun, and will help staff feel confident and prepared if these tools do become a mechanism for delivering online library services.

Perpetual beta

Once your new service launches, a wise idea is to treat it as a perpetual beta test. With the speed at which technology is moving and the number of new applications that launch seemingly on a daily basis, working with web technologies can feel like trying to hit a rapidly moving target. There's no better way of ensuring that you remain flexible and responsive to new developments, and in step with your users' expectations, than accepting that your service will to some degree never be out of the testing stage.

Once you have an active community established, they will be the first to tell you how they think your application or service can be improved. Quite often this will be a natural part of the dialogue you have with your users; you'll see comments appearing in response to blog posts, or as part of a discussion thread, saying 'Wouldn't it be nice if...?' and suggesting a way that the service could be better. These kinds of comments should always be noted and, if enough users are demanding or hoping for the addition of a certain feature, its feasibility can be investigated.

In addition to *ad hoc* suggestions, it's also a good idea to solicit direct feedback from users on a regular (if not permanent) basis. Questions asking for users' opinions on new web services can be incorporated into any surveys that your library typically carries out at certain times, such as large-scale telephone surveys. Online survey tools such as Survey Monkey (www.surveymonkey.com) make it relatively simple to set up a specific online survey that can be linked from the front page of your blog, wiki or other service asking for opinions. A simple Likert scale asking users to rate the service on a scale of 1 to 10, with an open comment box underneath, is quick and easy for users to fill out and can provide very valuable data on whether your service is effective.

Ask staff for feedback, too. As both users and administrators of the service, their input can be extremely important when it comes to service improvement. The staff responsible for day-to-day moderation and management can tell you exactly where hotspots and problems are occurring and which back-end processes seem inefficient and time-consuming.

Ongoing collection of feedback from staff and patrons allows you to monitor areas that are repeatedly identified as being problems and/or in need of improvement. These might be new features, interface changes or simply suggestions for a different approach at the top level – for example, letting members of a virtual book club nominate suggestions for the next book for discussion, rather than having a library staff member select the book. If you spot trends in terms of feature requests or process improvements, a good way of ensuring buy-in before making any changes is to give the choice back to the community: conduct a quick poll or survey asking if this is definitely something they would like to see implemented. If a majority answer yes, you can go ahead and make the change.

Committing to a culture of continuous improvement and perpetual beta means that you can remain flexible and responsive to these kinds of requests. It's also an excellent way of ensuring that you keep up with the technological changes that are important to your user base, and most importantly that you continue to remain relevant to your community.

The checklist

Any time you consider implementing a new web service, keep this checklist to hand and run through it. These are all the major points that you should consider to ensure a successful launch.

Plan in advance.

- State your goals.
- Define your success measures.
- Consider the impact on library policies.
- Build buy-in and organizational support.

Choose your tools wisely.

- Ensure they add value to library services.
- Consider workload: technical, content and moderation.
- Mash up or build up?
- Be strategic; avoid fads.
- Assess for sustainability.
- Assess for capacity.
- Play it safe: start small.

Implement successfully.

- Create policies.
- Create workflow plan.
- Launch for a pilot period.
- Monitor response.
- Monitor workload.
- Refine policies and plans.
- Seek feedback and input.
- Adopt a process of continuous evaluation and improvement.

Notes

1 LibraryThing (undated) 'Terms of use'; available at: *www.librarything.com/privacy#terms* (accessed: 3 August 2008).

6

Conclusion

Embracing the firehose

Thousands of words have been expended on the value (or lack of value, depending on the author's perspective) of user-generated content. It's certainly true that when every opinion has a platform and every voice a space to broadcast, there's a danger of becoming overwhelmed by the resulting cacophony.

But it's also true that the end result is not necessarily cultural devastation. As individual users become more aware of the nature of information distribution, they also become more aware of the inherent pitfalls. When your average teenager knows perfectly well that they can go to Vox or LiveJournal and start a blog where they can post whatever thoughts they're currently feeling directly to the internet, they're very much aware that other people can do exactly the same thing. The internet doesn't train us simply to swallow every passing opinion that we read; in fact, it breeds a more determined skepticism and a more critical eye than ever before. The thing about living in a changing environment is that it's not just our surroundings that alter: we evolve too.

The read/write web is not going to go away. The doors are open now, and trying to shut them is an exercise in futility. All the hand-wringing in the world will not put the collective output of the web's millions of bloggers back in the box. It's far better, and more productive, to accept that this is the environment in which we operate now, and to be open to the possibilities that it creates.

For librarians, it may seem at times as though user-generated content is threatening the very heart of what we do. It used to be so simple: we went to library school and were taught exactly how to recognize authority, and with that understanding learned how to control and organize information. There is simply no way that we can apply our traditional notions of authority, as is, to the internet. To do so runs the risk of throwing out the baby with the bathwater: discarding millions of pages of factually correct, well-researched, interesting content simply because they weren't created by someone with the appropriate letters after their name or experience in an industry.

This is said without any wish to detract from sources that do have the formal citations, whose authors do have the letters after their names. These qualifications and experience bring with them an unalterable value, easy to understand and trust, and that will never change. What we need to be wary of is clinging to that value to the exclusion of all else. We need to accept and understand that community experts can bring valid, relevant, accurate contributions to the information pool; that they are quite capable of enhancing the overall quality of this pool. They also bring a level of accessibility that makes their knowledge and opinions easy to disseminate and easy to share.

Embracing user-generated content is about celebrating the library as a true community space. It's about welcoming community expertise, that collective wisdom of the crowds. It's about understanding that knowledge comes from conversation and dialogue, and that providing a space for this dialogue to take place is a part of our role as the custodians of community memory. It's a way for us to engage more directly with our users, to encourage them to participate freely and openly in dialogue with the library. More than anything else, it's a way for us to ensure we remain relevant in a world where the pace of change grows faster every day.

What happens next?

Technologically, that pace of change is now so rapid that it's very hard to predict what the future will hold. Every week brings a host of new web apps that can be used to enhance content, share content, discover and connect. Companies and individual entrepreneurs vie to become the next YouTube or Facebook, to be the one to offer the next big thing. With the best minds of a generation hooked into the net and eager to experiment, even the best new for-fee products are only around for the blink of an eye before someone else launches a free or open source version. Finding the killer app is more and more about the things that make a product or piece of software truly unique: either the content it contains or the value-add service it provides. It may not even be about making money as much as making its creator's name known.

Web 3.0 certainly offers some very interesting potential for change, particularly if products such as Powerset and Twine achieve their full potential. True semantic search and discovery will make the hooks that we throw into the internet to pull back the information we need far more accurate and effective. They will make it considerably easier to avoid the dross, the seething mass of web content that is either inaccurate or irrelevant and that currently gets in the way of the information we really need. Reliable natural language searching will change the way our patrons retrieve information from the internet once again, and there may be less need for the kind of information literacy skills and training that are in such high demand now.

What we may find instead is that we ourselves, the library professionals, assume a greater role in the creation of content, weaving what we know into the threads on Twine and providing the quality information captured by the new and more effective searching hooks. We may find ourselves becoming the power behind the throne, working with the companies that are producing the new semantic search tools to build new taxonomies and folksonomies, new schemata for organizing and retrieving information. It's hard to say, because right now we don't know exactly how the semantic web is going to evolve. A year from now, it may have changed direction completely.

These are the things we do know, that we can say for sure about the future.

We will need to be responsive without being reactive. We will need to move faster than we have in the past, to be flexible and adaptable and ready to seize the new opportunities. We will need to develop an agile service model that allows us to pilot projects swiftly, evaluate them effectively, discard them if necessary and build on them if they succeed. We will need to accept that the changing technology and information environment will continue to reshape our profession, and develop the change management skills to handle this to our own and our patrons' advantage. We will need to build this understanding into our strategic planning, our policies and our organizational goals. We will continue to be excited by new technologies, new opportunities and a whole new world of possibility.

Index

FSC
www.fsc.org
MIX
Papier | Fördert gute Waldnutzung
FSC® C083411

Kolibri 360 GmbH
Ferdinand-Jühlke-Straße 7
99095 Erfurt, Deutschland
produktsicherheit@kolibri360.de